GOODBYE
CANADA?

GOODBYE CANADA?

WRITTEN BY

PAUL KEMP

EDITED BY

CRISS HAJEK

Benson & Hedges

BREAKOUT EDUCATIONAL NETWORK
IN ASSOCIATION WITH
DUNDURN PRESS
TORONTO · OXFORD

Publisher: Inta D. Erwin
Copy-editor: Maggie MacDonald, First Folio Resource Group
Designer: Bruna Brunelli, Brunelli Designs
Production Editor: Amanda Stewart, First Folio Resource Group
Printer: Webcom

National Library of Canada Cataloguing in Publication Data

Kemp, Paul
    Goodbye Canada?/by Paul Kemp; edited by Criss Hajek

One of the 16 vols. and 14 hours of video which make up the
    underground royal commission report.
Includes bibliographical references and index
ISBN 1-55002-421-3

    1. Canada — Foreign economic relations — United States. 2. United
States — Foreign economic relations — Canada. 3. Canada — Economic
conditions — 1991– I. Hajek, Criss II. Title. III. Title: underground
royal commission report.

HC115.K44 2002   330.971'0648   C2002-902301-7

1   2   3   4   5   07   06   05   04   03

Printed and bound in Canada.
Printed on recycled paper. ♻
www.dundurn.com

Portions of the transcripts that appear in *Goodbye Canada?* are featured in the Stornoway Productions television documentary *Canada's Brain Drain*, which was broadcast nationally numerous times on Global Television and Prime between 1999 and 2002.

Exclusive Canadian broadcast rights for the *underground royal commission* report

intelligent television
Check your cable or satellite listings for telecast times

Visit the *urc* Web site link at:
www.ichanneltv.com

The *underground royal commission* Report

Since September 11, 2001, there has been an uneasy dialogue among Canadians as we ponder our position in the world, especially vis à vis the United States. Critically and painfully, we are re-examining ourselves and our government. We are even questioning our nation's ability to retain its sovereignty.

The questions we are asking ourselves are not new. Over the last 30 years, and especially in the dreadful period of the early 1990s, leading up to the Quebec referendum of 1995, inquiries and Royal commissions, one after another, studied the state of the country. What *is* new is that eight years ago, a group of citizens looked at this parade of inquiries and commissions and said, "These don't deal with the real issues." They wondered how it was possible for a nation that was so promising and prosperous in the early 60s to end up so confused, divided, and troubled. And they decided that what was needed was a different kind of investigation — driven from the grassroots 'bottom,' and not from the top. Almost as a provocation, this group of people, most of whom were affiliated with the award winning documentary-maker, Stornoway Productions, decided to do it themselves — and so was born the *underground royal commission*!

What began as a television documentary soon evolved into much more. Seven young, novice researchers, hired right out of university, along with a television crew and producer, conducted interviews with people in government, business, the military and in all walks of life, across the country. What they discovered went beyond anything they had expected. The more they learned, the larger the implications grew. The project continued to evolve and has expanded to include a total of 23 researchers over the last several years. The results are the 14 hours of video and 16 books that make up the first interim report of the *underground royal commission*.

So what *are* the issues? The report of the *underground royal commission* clearly shows us that regardless of region, level of government, or political party, we are operating under a wasteful system ubiquitously lacking in accountability. An ever-weakening connection between the electors and the elected means that we are slowly and irrevocably losing our right to know our government. The researchers' experiences demonstrate that it is almost impossible for a member of the public, or in most cases, even for a member of Parliament, to actually trace how our tax dollars are spent. Most disturbing is the fact that our young people have been stuck with a crippling IOU that has effectively hamstrung their future. No wonder, then, that Canada is not poised for reaching its potential in the 21st century.

The *underground royal commission* report, prepared in large part by and for the youth of Canada, provides the hard evidence of the problems you and I may long have suspected. Some of that evidence makes it clear that, as ordinary Canadians, we are every bit as culpable as our politicians — for our failure to demand accountability, for our easy acceptance of government subsidies and services established without proper funding in place, and for the disservice we have done to our young people through the debt we have so blithely passed on to them. But the real purpose of the *underground royal commission* is to ensure that we better understand how government processes work and what role we play in them. Public policy issues must be understandable and accessible to the public if they are ever to be truly addressed and resolved. The *underground royal commission* intends to continue pointing the way for bringing about constructive change in Canada.

— Stornoway Productions

Books in the *underground royal commission* Report

"Just Trust Us"

The Chatter Box
The Chance of War
Talking Heads Talking Arms: (3 volumes)
No Life Jackets
Whistling Past the Graveyard
Playing the Ostrich

Days of Reckoning
Taking or Making Wealth
Guardians on Trial
Goodbye Canada?
Down the Road Never Travelled
Secrets in High Places
On the Money Trail

Does Your Vote Count?
A Call to Account
Reflections on Canadian Character

14 hours of videos also available with the *underground royal commission* report.
Visit Stornoway Productions at www.stornoway.com for a list of titles.

GOODBYE
CANADA?

CONTENTS

BIOGRAPHIES

INTERVIEWEES

BIOGRAPHIES:

DAN AYKROYD ♣
Actor, comedian, writer and a recent recipient of the Order of Canada. Dan Aykroyd left Canada for opportunities in New York with *Saturday Night Live* and has furthered his stellar career within the Hollywood film industry.
CANADIAN

LAURIE BAGGIO ♣
Vancouver-based entrepreneur and president of Helicon, a start-up company that develops Internet video games. Laurie has been fighting to expand a company dealing with interactive Internet programs and has lost employees and funding to the United States. Like many others, he feels the powerful professional pull of America and that personal tug of the country in which he was born.
CANADIAN

JANICE BASSO ❀

One of the organizers of the job recruiting fair at Bingemans Convention Centre. The fair was sponsored by the University of Guelph, University of Waterloo, Sir Wilfrid Laurier University and Conestoga College and brought together over 750 employer representatives with over 3,000 university students.

CANADIAN

DAVID J. BLUMBERG 🇺🇸

President, Blumberg Capital — a venture capital firm operating out of San Francisco, Calif. David Blumberg spent many years as a resident of Canada and provides important insight into the financial perspectives of both Canadians and Americans.

AMERICAN

JIM BURNS ❀

Chairman, Great West Life Co. Inc. and former deputy chairman, Power Corporation Canada.

CANADIAN

NOEL DESAUTELS ❀

Noel Desautels, a professional business consultant, is the longest-standing executive of the Harvard Business School Club of Toronto. As a Canadian recruiter for Harvard Business School, he promotes Harvard to bright, young Canadian students interested in academic challenge. He also leads an initiative to encourage top Harvard MBA graduates to return to Canada by matching the students with employers in Canada.

CANADIAN

DON DEVORETZ ❀

Don Devoretz is the co-director of the Centre of Excellence for the Study of Immigration and a professor of economics at Simon Fraser University in Burnaby, B.C. Dr. Devoretz's main writings have been on the economic impact of immigration in the labour market and the brain drain from Canada. His work has been reported in over 50 peer-reviewed articles.

CANADIAN

MICHELLE DONATO ♣

Dr. Michelle Donato left Canada to train as a bone marrow transplant specialist with expertise in ovarian cancer at the prestigious M. D. Anderson Cancer Center in Houston. She now works there with several internationally respected Canadian medical professionals.
CANADIAN

STEVE GOLDSMITH ♣

A University of Waterloo graduate and recruiter for Trilogy, a software company based in Austin, Tex.
CANADIAN

JOE GOODMAN

Joe Goodman is professor emeritus, Department of Electrical Engineering at Stanford University in Palo Alto, Calif. As a professor at Stanford since 1962, he has also served as a director of several Silicon Valley corporations in the photonics and optics field, including Optivision Inc., which he co-founded.
AMERICAN

EVE HESSELROTH

American recruiter for Trilogy, a software company based in Austin, Tex.
AMERICAN

BRENT HOLIDAY ♣

Founding partner of Greenstones Venture Partners in Vancouver, B.C., Brent Holiday has been a venture capitalist since 1994. His company focuses on seed-stage financing of start-up companies. Brent also writes a biweekly column called "Something Ventured" for BC-technology.com, providing insight into the demands of the new economy on Canada's West Coast industry.
CANADIAN

BEN KELLY ♣

University of Guelph student and president of the Commerce Society in 1999 at the University of Guelph.
CANADIAN

MARIE KLAWE ✤
Dean of science at the University of British Columbia. A Canadian who joined the UBC faculty in 1988 after living a good part of her working life in the U.S. Her position at UBC has given her a spectacular view of the pressures that are mounting on Canadian researchers both inside and outside of universities.
CANADIAN

BOB MILLER ▤
Bob Miller is the vice provost for intellectual property and technology transfer at the University of Washington in Seattle. Bob previously worked at the University of British Columbia for 22 years and gave up his tenure there to join the University of Washington in an innovative role that advocates the university's commercialization of knowledge.
AMERICAN

HARRIS MILLER ▤
Harris Miller is the president of the Information Technology Association of America (ITAA), located in Arlington, Va., just across the river from Washington, D.C. The ITAA represents the broad spectrum of public policy issues pertaining to the U.S.'s world-leading informa-tion and technology companies and industries.
AMERICAN

JACK MINTZ ✤
Currently the president and CEO of the C. D. Howe Institute based in Toronto, Jack Mintz is also the Arthur Andersen Professor of Taxation at the Joseph L. Rotman School of Management at the University of Toronto. He was commissioned in 1997 by the Department of Finance in Ottawa to do an in-depth analysis of Canada's tax system.
CANADIAN

MIKE OKINCHA ✤
A graduate of the University of Waterloo's electrical engineering department, Mike also has an MBA from Wilfrid Laurier University. One month after graduating he moved to Silicon Valley to work in the optics field.
CANADIAN

MICHAEL OKINCHA, SR. ✤
Mike Okincha's father, Michael Okincha, Sr., is employed as an executive with Rogers in Toronto.
CANADIAN

DAVID PRITCHARD 🇺🇸
Interviewed in Redmond, Wash., David Pritchard is the director of recruiting for the Microsoft Corporation.
AMERICAN

SHEILA SPENCE ✤
Director of development, Primedia Inc., New York City. Sheila graduated from the University of Western Ontario with a business degree, is a former Wall Street banker with Soloman Bros. in both New York and Hong Kong and holds an MBA from acclaimed Harvard University.
CANADIAN

PAUL SWINWOOD ✤
Paul Swinwood is the president of the Software Human Resource Council based in Ottawa. The council has been looking at the issue of the brain drain for the last few years to build data for a major study of who is leaving the country, their skill set, the supply and demand and how the people who are leaving are faring.
CANADIAN

CHRIS TAYLOR ✤
President of Gas Powered Games based in Kirkland, a suburb of Seattle Wash., Chris Taylor is a Vancouver-born international superstar of video-game design who now employs 30 young game developers at the business he started on his own in 1997.
CANADIAN

PETER WOLKEN 🇺🇸
General partner, AVI Capital. Peter Wolken has been a venture capitalist in Silicon Valley since 1982 and originally worked with Intel founder Bob Noyce. He formed AVI Capital in 1982 and has since raised over half a billion dollars and invested in notable companies

such as Apple, 3Com, S3, Ask Systems, Extreme Networks and LGC
Wireless.

AMERICAN

CHAPTER I

A WAKE-UP CALL

I DO NOT WANT TO be taken as being flippant or off-handed, but I came to write this book with a queasy feeling in the pit of my gut telling me Canada, the nation, is in trouble. I know some readers will dismiss me as a typical "Canadian doomsayer," or claim that statements like this have been made for decades and that Canada is more resilient than this book propounds. I believe I will prove those people wrong.

I have purposefully entitled this book *Goodbye Canada?* with a question mark because I think the kind of trouble I describe is the kind of trouble we, as a country, can rectify. The information presented here represents seven years of firsthand study of our government and its institutions, and those who are not willing to look at the evidence of Canada's troubles are dooming it to become a further weakened state. This book discloses what I have learned and is my attempt to give Canada a wake-up call.

So here we go …

It is not often that we get a chance to be a part of something important and meaningful that helps us understand the country we live in.

Three years ago, as a 28-year-old Canadian, I did get an opportunity to witness my country in a refreshing and original way. In early 1999 I was tasked with examining Canada — *its strengths and weaknesses* — from the outside looking in. I was given the responsibility of determining why so many young and educated university graduates were opting to live and work outside of Canada in various parts of the United States. At the time it seemed there was a subtle shift in the attitude of young people toward their role in Canadian society. A subtle shift, yes, but from my standpoint, an increasingly evident one. Based on that hunch, I was to report back in the form of a television documentary about a subject that was sneaking under the radar screen of most journalists and Canadian policy makers at the time. The goal was to have the documentary, tentatively entitled *Should I Stay or Should I Go*, broadcast nationally on Global Television. This was a weighty assignment to be sure, but one I now believe has allowed me to draw some weighty conclusions.

Where should I begin to tell this story, or more appropriately, what was the perspective of my country as seen by those who have left it? Thankfully, I was not starting from square one in this assignment. I was not just given a digital camera and told to go shoot reams of footage down in the United States and hope for the best. No, it started a little more innocently, several years earlier.

Back in 1994, shortly after I graduated from the University of Manitoba, a Toronto-based film producer approached me about getting involved with a group of other young Canadians who would chronicle for television, their journey across the country in search of the root causes of Canada's $600-billion debt. It sounded like a good proposition at the time. First of all, with my freshly minted Bachelor of Arts degree, I was looking for an exciting job (just any job really) and this clearly fit the bill. Secondly, and more to the point, cast your mind back to 1994; it was not a great year. The economy was just coming out of a pit of despair; our country was in debt up to its eyeballs; the Canada Pension Plan was looking ghastly; constitutionally the country was at an impasse; and morally, people in Canada, particularly people my age, were incredibly disenchanted with our political leaders. Yet I had to admit, despite my economics and political studies background, I did not fully understand why. To go around the country to ascertain some answers seemed like a calling at that time. So I said "yes" to the film producer and began my "cross-country schooling" on the problems facing Canada.

Although I would love to jot down everything I found on that three-year investigation through 10 provinces while conducting nearly 200 interviews, it would take weeks to do my discoveries justice. Editing the nearly 150 hours of raw material down to three hours was back-breaking work. The results of our journey were summed up in a three-part documentary series entitled *Days of Reckoning*, which aired on television in 1998. It gave Canadians an important glimpse of the country over the past 35 years and provided a context for the political malaise that struck Canada in the mid-1990s.

Why *Days of Reckoning* was so important was that our group investigated almost every current issue ailing our country in the mid-1990s. The issues we tackled went from the history of Canada's social safety net to the fracturing of the Canadian federal state. We looked at unemployment insurance in P.E.I. and the Canadian Wheat Board in Saskatchewan. We critiqued the troubled Workers' Compensation Board in Ontario and the demise of the fishery in Newfoundland. We discovered how the Canada Pension Plan (CPP) was a generational time bomb waiting to go off for younger people and employers. We witnessed how today, despite Canada's current tax-cut environment, Canadians will see payroll taxes double over 15 years to cover the CPP budget shortfall — all to deal with an avoidable mess our leaders ignored for nearly 30 years. We substantiated the causes of government debt and why it had amassed so greatly since the 1970s. We explored how government monopolies affected our economy and why dying industries were fruitlessly subsidized for decades. We saw what government loan guarantees, used to save old economy jobs, can do to companies and small towns across Canada. We observed how job-creation programs were used as valuable political tools, yet often produced little evidence of actually creating jobs. We began to understand a seismic shift in public attitudes in Canada toward government, where everyday law-abiding Canadians began to do everything they could to avoid taxes and increasingly joined the underground economy. We also probed our political system and noted the increased role unelected interest groups and lobbyists had on influencing our government structures. Ultimately, and perhaps most importantly, we began to understand how accountability, or a lack thereof, was affecting our cherished government institutions and the very nature of our Parliament itself.

Notably, we did not address any of these critical Canadian issues in isolation. We recognized that most media outlets dealt with the pressing topics of the day by simply doing a quick article in a newspaper or a three-minute news segment on TV. This of course seemed ridiculous to us when trying to understand the complex nature of problems facing our nation. No one can understand deep-rooted problems without understanding their background and history. So we tried to build connections between issues in order to understand the real political economy in which Canadians live their day-to-day lives.

Now before you declare that there was no way anyone (especially me) could possibly have understood all the issues I have just outlined in an in-depth way, I will agree with you. But only insofar as to say I knew I did not have all the answers, not even close to all of them. However, what I was developing was a first-person account of my own country and a context in which to look at its political malaise. I was witnessing the symptoms of its political sickness everywhere. Not many people are given such a firsthand education.

When it came time to look at the next stage of my investigation — to understand how highly talented people critically appraise the place they came from — the questions seemed easier, more to the point. I immediately recognized that Canadians were making their life decisions based on the opportunities presented to them, and if the opportunities were in the U.S., so be it. Did these same people understand the link between how Canada governs itself and the personal choices they were making? I needed to see the connection.

During my journey, I spent significant amounts of time in the United States, in Houston, in New York, in Boston, in Los Angles, all over Silicon Valley, in the Seattle area and in Washington, D.C. I interviewed approximately 100 former Canadians who now reside in the United States. I also observed many current American business leaders and entrepreneurs.

When I started to look at Canada through the eyes of people who had left, it forced me to open my eyes to a world I really did not comprehend. Sure, I understood that many of my friends in their mid-20s were opting to take jobs in the U.S. and that this was a growing trend. However, I wanted to ascertain if this was just an anecdotal phenomenon or if the chatter of "better jobs and opportunity in the U.S." was a reality. What did expatriate Canadians think were the strengths of Canada, or its weaknesses? Did they even care?

This is not a book designed to champion the U.S., nor is it a précis of all that is wrong with Canada. It is a glimpse at what real Canadians and, most importantly, the innovative young players in the growing parts of the U.S. economy think ... about their lives, the future of the nation they now call home and the country they used to call home.

I also knew I had to understand my country from a young person's perspective, not from the older crowd who had familiar notions of what Canada is or is not. The younger crowd would not be burdened by nostalgia or bias about what makes Canada strong or weak. This book, therefore, uses their words about Canada as they see it. I asked the questions, focused the discussion, but those interviewed provided the answers.

I have also furnished a few personal anecdotes to enable the story to flow more smoothly and provide insights as to why certain people were interviewed.

The first section of the book focuses on a number of young people who decided to leave Canada. These people were selected after many phone calls, meetings and research because they were representative of people who actually made the move south of the border. I wanted to focus on people who recently graduated, as well as those who had been in the U.S. for various amounts of time. I chose a New York Wall Street high-flier, a Seattle video-games developer and entrepreneur, a high-tech engineer in Silicon Valley, a cancer specialist in Houston and a Canadian comedian in Hollywood.

Chapter II

Should I Stay or Should I Go?

Contributors in this section:

Dan Aykroyd	*Mike Okincha*
Laurie Baggio	*Michael Okincha, Sr.*
Michelle Donato	*Sheila Spence*
Brent Holiday	*Chris Taylor*

PAUL:

BEFORE I BEGIN TO OUTLINE my story of discovery, there are two things I should make clear.

Firstly, I have not cluttered this book with any graphs, charts or statistical analysis to prove the points I have made. I have only presented the evidence that I personally gathered throughout the United States and Canada. The interviews you are about to read are all firsthand accounts of what I have seen and heard.

Secondly, these words are what the interviewees said during on-camera interviews. Each person has his or her own way of speaking and his or her own style of responding to my questions. Therefore, while reading the various chapters, be forewarned that the style of writing may change slightly throughout. Perhaps it would be a good idea to envision these people speaking on television as their words are presented.

With that said, let's proceed …

Mike Okincha was one of my first interviewees and I conducted several in-depth interviews with him over an eight-month period. Two of these interviews were on camera for the television show — one of them in Oakville, Ont., his hometown, the other in Sunnyvale, Calif., in Silicon Valley, his new home. I even tracked Mike to Pearson Airport in Toronto to witness him saying goodbye to his family, his girlfriend and Canada, perhaps for good.

MIKE OKINCHA, GRADUATE ♣

When I started to think about a career, I realized if I were a star performer in a Canadian company, I would only get paid the same as the mediocre performers in exactly the same job. So everybody with the same job designation would be paid within a narrow band. It would not be important how well or how poorly I performed; I would get paid based on where I ranked in the company.

Therefore, if I were going to be paid for being a star performer, I would have to go to the United States to be rewarded. If I stayed in Canada, I would be recognized as a good employee but the financial rewards and potential for advancement would not be there. Even if I did not want to be advanced, I would not be rewarded for doing a job well. The only incentive that Canadian companies offer is to try and move you up into management or into a higher rank. Sometimes that is not your career path.

I want to go for the gusto. I want to build companies that are stellar performers, I want to be at the leading edge of things, I want to be where the action is. Whether I do that in Canada or in the U.S. does not matter. I am going to go wherever it is geographically the easiest to achieve those goals.

The education I received was fantastic. I spoke to people at Massachusetts Institute of Technology (MIT) and students at Harvard University and major schools all over the world, and Canadian students were at least as good, if not better in some respects, than just about every other school. My education was excellent and that was one of the biggest attractions for the people in the United States.

From a business perspective, I have managed to pay a very low price for my education. Taxpayers and everyone I know would argue that I have been subsidized by their money, and that is one of the unfortunate features of the system. Now I have a motivated self-interest to make the best use of my education.

If I can do that in Canada, then I stay in Canada. If there is a better place, then I will look at going there as an option. The fact that I received this subsidized education really does not influence me a whole lot. I did not choose to have that subsidy; I was born into the system and because I have made use of it, I do not think I should be penalized or held responsible for taking advantage of what already exists.

Everywhere there is a demand for people of quality and for people with good skills. That demand does not stop at any national border, nor at any sea border. It is worldwide. People want to make the most of their skills. We want to earn the highest salaries and get the best opportunities. If we can do that somewhere other than Canada, then there are no barriers preventing us from leaving.

PAUL:

Mike was a unique person to contact for several reasons. First of all, he was a 24-year-old graduate from the University of Waterloo's esteemed engineering program and held a Master of Business Administration degree from Wilfrid Laurier University. In other words, he was a very heavily educated Canadian. Not only was Mike educated, he was also incredibly entrepreneurial. When I stated I wanted to look into some of the reasons Silicon Valley was so appealing and why it had become so successful in helping finance upstart companies, Mike was immediately interested in the potential financiers and venture capitalists I may have contacted. Clearly he had his own plans for some sort of venture in the future. In fact, throughout university Mike had operated his own computer consulting company and employed up to five people. He had closed the company down to accept his new job in San Jose.

Despite his young age, Mike was reflective about his choice to go south to work in the digital optics field with a cutting-edge technology company. The tech boom in the U.S. was taking off and Mike wanted to be part of it. What interested me most were the reasons he was going. He opened my eyes as to why Canada was losing people like him because of some of the inherent difficulties in this country's corporate culture.

MIKE OKINCHA, GRADUATE ✤

One of my problems here was finding mentors, people that I could work with to develop my skills. These people are even in greater demand than me and so they are leaving faster. As the number of people that I can really learn anything from is diminishing, I have no choice. Either I stay

24

here and become stagnant and stale in my own skills, or I move to wherever the experts are and try and learn from them.

Canada has not developed a large number of leading-edge, technological companies and those that do come here find the environment more hostile than in the United States.

Canada is a bit of a desert in a bureaucracy in that sense, if you want to look at it in a ecosystem kind of way. There are many companies with divisions all over the world and major technological companies come to Canada to try to start a division here. They find the tax system is difficult and it is hard to find qualified or particularly talented people. They find a whole series of hostile environmental factors that act as a disincentive for them to stay.

Canadian companies are big on pay equity and on equal treatment and equal opportunity. I realized that a person in a particular job would be paid the same as everyone else in that same job regardless of whether they were a mediocre performer or a particularly stellar employer or particularly stellar employee.

I am really not sure what Canada could do to keep me. I am looking for a place where I can be recognized for my skills and for my drive and ambition and my abilities. I am also looking for people with the skills and abilities to be mentors to me and help me develop my own abilities to a higher level. I do not think I would find that in Canada.

PAUL:

As Mike was one of my early interviewees, I was only just opening my mind up to the fact that he was stating things that would later play a significant role in the story I would tell. In fact, his views on mentorship by more skilled employees, the attraction of top people to specialized areas of the economy and the differences in what he called "pay equity" within the high-tech culture of the U.S. would later be repeated to me literally dozens of times.

Mike also hit a chord when he talked about his sense of loyalty to Canada. He was the first, in what would be a cast of many, who I perceived as having an odd, possibly generationally unique sense of Canadian patriotism. Post–World War II Canadians and their children may have had a mythic sense of Canada, perhaps well deserved 40 or 50 years ago, but today's new generation seemed more apt to express loyalty to family and friends in Canada. Their patriotism rarely went beyond the local level. Almost like clockwork, most people I talked to paid lip service to Canadian values. They related support for the goals of medicare and Canada's social safety net being a reflection of Canada's "softer, gentler" society, yet clearly their actions — living, working and paying taxes in the U.S. — did not seem to match those words. Most seemed focused on their individual lifestyle and work choices with little sense of "country" on a grand scale, either American or Canadian.

Mike Okincha's words to this effect were typical.

MIKE OKINCHA, GRADUATE ♣

I do not think that the fact that I am a Canadian has a major effect on whether or not I move to another country. I have friends who have moved to just about every part of the world and no one holds a grudge against them for having moved to another country because it is seen as the best thing for that individual.

I do not think there is any real Canadian patriotism per se. With the internationalization going on in the world, the European union forming and NAFTA agreements, the borders between countries are really being broken down. This sense of being from a particular country in a lot of ways is being eroded. The fact that I am Canadian by birth does not really tie me to staying within Canada. I am proud to be a Canadian, but that does not mean I am going to stay in Canada all of my life.

The allegiance to Canada is stronger amongst older people. The sense of patriotism, because of the various wars that people have experienced, was much stronger.

My leaving Canada should not be interpreted as being unpatriotic. I am really doing what is best for me personally. In a few years I may choose to move back to Canada, bringing the skills that I have developed. In some ways it may be best for Canada for me to go and get experience in other countries, develop an expertise and bring it back.

PAUL:

Is an allegiance to one's country enough to combat the war on talent? They may want to come back, they may pine for their old neighbourhoods, their friends, their families, but in this day and age do individuals care about the border anymore?

I was clearly hearing a more global, yet individual, attitude being fostered by expatriate Canadians throughout the U.S. Interestingly enough, what I saw was a change in attitude back home in Canada as well, even in some of the Canadian families of the people I interviewed. Mike's father, Michael Okincha, Sr., seemed to confirm that attitude.

MICHAEL OKINCHA, SR., FATHER ♣

Talk about hockey, talk about any other professional area, and you will find people migrating to those opportunities. It is a natural occurrence. And I think to artificially try to stifle that is not natural. What are you going to do, keep them hostage?

There are a bunch of Canadians trying to make their way in this world and I am pleased to hear them staying together as a class. That creates the sense of camaraderie, the fraternity of professionals. I would like to see the government encourage people to gain new experience and bring it back. I believe that is part of the whole process and I would like to see more action in that area. I have been trying to hire some expertise, some management in a group where I work and I am having a really tough time because of the drain of technical people into California, into Microsoft and so on. As a result, I have been trying to fill a position for the last six months that I thought should be fairly easy to fill. The position offers an attractive salary and so on, but people are becoming contractors and they are moving south. There are virtual companies using the Internet for servicing customers and I am having difficulty finding somebody locally. I have to bring up the ante and become more flexible to fill those roles.

PAUL:

As I navigated the waters of national allegiance, borders and loyalty to one's homeland, the high-tech industries seemed to be where the greatest risk of losing our citizens to the U.S. existed. However, it became apparent that other areas of our economy, such as finance, law, health and entertainment, were also heavily affected by Canadians heading south.

As health care is of paramount political importance in Canada, it was necessary to talk to young research doctors about their views on mentorship, funding of health care and why the U.S. research facilities were attracting Canadians. When I came across a column in *The Globe and Mail* about Houston's M. D. Anderson Hospital, one of the top cancer research and treatment facilities in the U.S., I made some calls.

I got in touch with a number of Canadians advancing their medical careers in Houston. Through Susan Spence-Wach, a Canadian who worked in the public relations department, I discovered just what a special place M. D. Anderson was. Susan said, "The singular focus here at M. D. Anderson and our mission is the elimination of cancer. That gives everyone that works in this institution a singular purpose and mission, and that is why we are here. If you have cancer, we are your best hope."

It was an impressive statement to say the least and gave me a taste of what I would find during my time in Houston. As the person who informally organized "Canadian Club" dinners for expatriates looking for the occasional connection to back home, Susan Spence-Wach put me in touch with 19 Canadians now working in the cancer field in Houston. She organized one of these dinners for our film crew and helped make my stay in Houston very eye-opening.

M. D. Anderson was a huge organization with 8,000 employees in all areas of research, patient care, the medical professions, nursing and support staff. When I looked at all those resources and all that expertise concentrating on cancer, it was clear that M. D. Anderson had an advantage in terms of what can be done to conquer the disease. To put it in perspective, the research budget for the M. D. Anderson hospital area in Houston was greater than the Medical Research Council of Canada budget and the National Cancer Institute's budget for all of Canada combined.

When I met a 30-year-old francophone cancer specialist from Montreal, this point was driven home. Dr. Michelle Donato advised that if I really wanted to understand the attraction of M. D. Anderson, I should just spend a few days with her on the bone marrow cancer wards. I did. Her story was illuminating.

DR. MICHELLE DONATO, CANCER SPECIALIST ✤

When I was training as a medical resident at the Royal Victoria Hospital in Montreal, I did some bone marrow transplants and was encouraged to try to learn more and become a bone marrow transplant specialist. There were a few centres in the U.S., like M. D. Anderson in Houston, doing a whole lot more, so I came down and interviewed. The place was incredible. I decided I would train as a transplanter, get the experience and then go back home. Then they asked me to stay and work for them and I had to stay, you know. The job was just too good. At the Royal Victoria Hospital we were probably doing about 20 bone marrow transplants a year. Here, at M. D. Anderson, we do over 500. The difference is enormous and the experience that I have gained here would have taken years, if not decades, at home.

At M. D. Anderson I am a full-time bone marrow transplanter, subspecializing in ovarian cancer and in breast cancer. Back home I would have been able to do general oncology and some bone marrow transplants, but I could not focus on one unique area and do research on that alone. Here essentially they let me do what I want. If I had a good idea and a plan, and if I could put it together and build up research, that was fine with them. In Montreal my purpose would be to fill a broader need as a general oncologist. Work-wise that is the main difference.

At 30 years old I am younger than most of my colleagues. The advantage of having been here is that, at age 30, I have seen hundreds of bone marrow transplants already, whereas at home I would probably have to be much older to have the amount of experience that I've gained here.

The opportunity I get from M. D. Anderson is really the opportunity to do the research that I want to do. That is something I was not getting when I went home to interview. They needed somebody to work in general oncology in the clinic and they needed somebody in the lab. I am not a lab person, I do not like the lab. I am good at what I do, and my colleagues at M. D. Anderson said, "Well, that's what you want to do and it sounds great. This is a new idea, it's a new project, we're not doing that, go for it." So that is what M. D. Anderson gave me and that is how our new ovarian cancer transplant program came about. We put the program together and it is going fabulously well. Patients are doing very well. If I have an idea, they will actually push me to develop my idea, not something they want me to work on. I think that is how we are going to make progress.

M. D. Anderson is a state institution, not private practice. I am salaried, and essentially I make the same money that I would be making at home as an attending physician at a big university hospital. The cost of living down here is overall about the same. The opportunity, though, is great.

I like Montreal. I like the city, I like my friends and it was difficult to leave. I understand that the Canadian taxpayer would feel that my education was subsidized and that I am not paying back by moving down here. I guess they do have a point, however, I hope that the research I am doing will benefit everybody. We have already published last year, we are publishing this year again and that is available to everybody. I am doing something here that I cannot do at home. The new therapies we develop here will benefit cancer patients everywhere, Canada and around the world. I hope I am paying back by that, a little bit.

"It is not the easier life that you search for but living life at the edge of all your possibilities." For now I think that is true. I hope so.

PAUL:

My next stop was Wall Street, where the financial world's best minds and money congregate. It is not a problem to track down top-rated Canadians in that part of New York City. Within three or four days of contacting the consulate, former school colleagues and business leaders in Canada, I had a Rolodex filled with potential Canadians to discuss the attraction of the Big Apple.

Although I suspected New York would be seen as a great city to live and work in, I certainly was not ready for the barrage of gratification, almost gloating, that came from the Canadians I met there. I quickly began to see New York City was unlike any other place in the world to advance one's profession. Was it even fair to compare the NYC working experience with that of cities in Canada? It was a good question for me, and one I knew I needed to explore because I also recognized that Canada, like it or not, was losing an exorbitant number of highly educated and talented people to New York.

One such talented individual was Sheila Spence, a 29-year-old University of Western Ontario graduate who also holds a Harvard University Master of Business Administration degree. Sheila had no difficulty adapting and melding into the culture of New York. She clearly felt at home as an imported New Yorker.

SHEILA SPENCE, BUSINESS DIRECTOR ♣

When I moved to New York it was because I was graduating from college and I was looking for something really fun and exciting to do. I would never have imagined when I moved here eight years ago that I would still be here after all this time. It was high-powered, fast-paced environments I was looking for, and I had no idea whether I would stay one year, two years, five years. I had no concept at all.

My parents always thought that I was entranced by New York City and very ambitious. If you asked them eight years ago, "Is Sheila coming back?" they might have said, "No, she's not." It took me a little while to get to that point myself. My parents have always been very supportive of my decisions in the jobs I have taken, in my education choices and where I decided to live and work.

I have worked in two industries in New York, investment banking and publishing. New York is the capital for both of those industries. The opportunity in my mind is just being at the global centre for where things happen. When you are at the heart of it, you are going to see more, learn more, get exposed to more people and to more interesting, cutting-edge activities. People who come to New York are looking for the challenge of being a part of the very leading edge.

New York has always been known as a centre for deal making, and our company has really made a mark as the mergers and acquisitions player in the publishing business. I work for a company called Primedia, which is a unique company in the publishing field. It is a real presence in the magazine business and information directories and publications. My job is to do acquisitions in the consumer magazine area. Some of our magazines are *New York*, *Seventeen* and *Modern Bride*. I have actually completed about 18 acquisitions since I started with the company, and most of those have been in the consumer magazine field. It has been very challenging and I am excited to be a part of it.

The business world really translates to the entrepreneurial activity here in the United States, and it is so much more extensive and developed with a greater history of entrepreneurial success and failure than in Canada. That is one of the things that attracts entrepreneurs or people with an entrepreneurial spirit to come here.

Nobody ever got anywhere by standing still and innovation has been very good for America. For example, Internet business and Internet activity is far more developed here than anywhere else in the world, and that is because people are willing to take the risks and invest the money and bring consumers into the Internet world.

One of the reasons I love New York so much is that everything is so accessible. For a large city everything is close. I live a block away from Central Park. I go running in the park. New York is probably the restaurant capital of the world and I do eat out a lot, like the stereotypical New Yorker does, and it is a great adventure every time you go to a new spot. The arts are fantastic. I am an opera fan and I go on a whim and you can do it here because there is so much selection.

New York has some drawbacks. Traffic can be unbearable, and it would be my number-one problem with the city. Also, every once in a while I cannot stand the fact that my apartment is so small.

In 10 years I would like to hope that the way I spend my time is a little different because I am working hard right now. I spend a lot of hours at my desk and on the road. I hope in 10 years I will have a little bit of a better mix between my personal life and work. In the end, though, if I have more time for personal life, then New York City is a great place to have it.

PAUL:

Not many cities can compete with the restaurants, nightlife and cultural energy of New York, but what about one thing that Sheila Spence kept mentioning — entrepreneurship? What drives the entrepreneur, the risk taker and the businessperson? Why can't new enterprises and successful businesses be blossoming in Canada instead of New York City?

It became clear that knowledge-based industries, or the "new economy," was an important focus for entrepreneurs. Although this was no news flash, this part of the economy seemed to attract many of the most innovative, visionary individuals in Canadian society.

In the following interviews I discussed the issue of entrepreneurship with two interesting individuals — still living in Canada — who had an immense amount of experience dealing in both the U.S. and Canadian economies.

Vancouver-based Laurie Baggio is an entrepreneur and strategic planner who sets goals for his business's development and future. He also spends much of his time looking for venture capital, which is money used for investment in projects that involve a high risk but offer the possibility of large profits. Brent Holiday is a Canadian venture capitalist investing in information technology, Internet and communications-related start-up or expanding companies.

As a novice to the start-up world, I wanted to discover what motivated the venture capitalist to invest in the early stages of a new business and how Canada is faring in this area overall.

LAURIE BAGGIO, ENTREPRENEUR ♣

We spent the last three years raising private money to work on some research and development technology called ERGO, a programming language we developed for the Internet. We started out with our friends and family, raised $100,000 in the first day, and basically that started us. We have some small investors and we are now looking at raising significant money from venture capitalists, about $3.5 million to $5 million (U.S.).

In Canada we spend most of our time looking for small-scale sources of income or government sources. Part of that reason is the culture. Basically the people that have access to smaller amounts of money, say under $1 million, take control of these small projects and have a short-term interest. They are looking at quarterly results or annual results. They are not thinking in terms of "Where can we be in three to five years?"

In the United States the attitude of the venture capitalists is such that they realize this company is going to lose money for five years in order to develop some really cool technology and maybe change an entire paradigm or way of operating in terms of selling a product or a service. But then the gains are enormous. Look at Yahoo and Amazon, for example. The things they are doing are fundamentally reshaping the way business is conducted.

Canadians in general, as a culture, think small. We can't afford to think that way anymore. When you look at countries like the United States, the attitude is to take on the whole world and succeed in a big way. It is very frustrating when Canadians still think in terms of what are we doing in Vancouver, what are we doing regionally, what's happening in British Columbia.

We have to start thinking about how to sell to everyone in the world. If you look at some of the larger companies, like Microsoft, you see that happening in a huge way, but a lot of start-ups think the same way as well. People in our society think about how they can sell to the storefronts locally, rather than how they can distribute to the entire planet.

Culturally, the new crop of kids today that are growing up with technology built in have a mindset for broader thinking. They do not think about all the rules and the way things should be done. They think, "Just do it." That is probably the biggest effect in terms of the brain drain. We are starting to see people who have the bigger ideas, the bigger concepts move to the United States and the thinking is not, "I want to do $100,000 in sales," it's "I want to do $100 million, I want to do $200 million in sales."

For my market to work I need to get my product out to as many people as possible to create a certain critical mass. This takes time to develop, but what I find is that the whole mindset in our economy and in our culture is to make money to survive this month.

What often happens in Canada is people take something to a certain point and then either sell out to a company from the United States or migrate their company to the U.S. so they can access larger capital markets.

The people that are actually going are key people for our industries, people that would make senior management for some of the best high-tech companies in the world. They are our best and brightest, people that could create a cornerstone for a high-tech industry. They are going because it is too difficult to deal with the infrastructure that we currently have in place.

In the U.S. I can go to a venture capitalist, pitch an idea and get a significant amount of money. Up here you basically have to be on the verge of selling the product before anybody would even consider speaking to you without taking over your entire company.

In Canada it's not just the venture capitalists that are at fault, it's not just the government, it's not just the taxation levels, it's not just the fact that the cream of our crop is basically heading to the States for bigger and better opportunities. It's ultimately the combination of all those different elements that hurts us. In the past we have been able to take advantage of commodities, forestry and mining — but there is no value there anymore. The only value added now is basically the brain power of the people you have in your economy. People are mobile and can move to where the money and the opportunities are unless you create that infrastructure across the board.

BRENT HOLIDAY, VENTURE CAPITALIST ✤

Basically, in Canada we have been a resource-based economy for so long, banks and other financiers think in terms of solid, tangible things, assets on the balance sheet, if you will. The economy is changing, obviously, and the fact is that a company's value is much more than what it has in its warehouse, especially in technology companies.

In Canada the mentality is slowly, glacially shifting toward what makes a knowledge-based economy work. Venture capital has emerged in Canada. Certainly there has been a lot of investment in early-stage technology and risk capital in general, but the banks are still the banks. The thinking flows from an overall mentality in government, in banks and everywhere else that knowledge-based companies are really confusing and too risky. You need a lot more venture capital to help these companies succeed because without the cash these companies are going to get to a certain stage and then not be able to make it. In fact, I would say that is really a problem in Canada. In many cases the existing risk capital has given these companies enough rope to hang themselves.

Canadian companies get enough money to get the product built and introduce it to the first few customers. However, when it's time to put money into marketing to get the product known and branded, risk capital in Canada tends to shy away. Investors do not want to put $20 million to $30 million into the company at this point. The company would then flounder and not have enough fuel to get to the stratosphere like many U.S.-based companies.

An early-stage technology company needs much more than just cash and money. It needs the support infrastructure, which is made up of lawyers, accountants, public relations and so forth — people that are not core to the company but that can really help the company succeed provided they know what they are doing. Also, the company needs access to talent. That is what you need in terms of what is called a critical mass.

Canadian management is usually made up of first-timers, and this is why Canadian companies have problems. A first-time entrepreneur does not have the experience or the knowledge base to really make a company turn on a dime. Experienced entrepreneurs know if that critical decision is coming; they know how agonizing that decision point is and what to do with the business.

When you have a large number of support and talented people in one place, a critical mass, it feeds upon itself. When people stay at a company for a short period of time and then flip to another, its not necessarily a bad thing. The individual takes the experience learned at one spot and moves it to another company. In Canada we are limited because a given company might be the only company in a certain geographic pocket that does a certain kind of business.

That, in a nutshell, is the problem in Canada. We are a geographically dispersed nation with pockets of talent in various cities — the Toronto area, the Ottawa area, the Kitchener-Waterloo triangle and then out West in Calgary and Vancouver. There are pockets of talent.

PAUL:

What I had learned at this juncture was making me reconsider many of the preconceptions I had formulated about my own country. Having grown up and lived in various parts of Canada, I began to think how a country's business or political culture is cultivated, or not. It made me wonder if Canadian institutions like our banking system, our tax system or our government regulations were helping or hindering our culture in the new world of business and entrepreneurs. The evidence was pointing to the latter.

As I spoke to people associated with some of the new and innovative companies in our economy, I wondered about my own inherent risk-averse nature. Was my disposition to prefer a secure job versus taking a risk to start my own company passed on to me by my risk-averse parents, or was I the offspring of my political system and the society it breeds?

One way to approach this question was through a kind of case study of the West Coast of Canada and the northwestern United States. Having spent a fairly significant amount of time in both Vancouver and Seattle, I wanted to explore the differences. I also wanted to learn about a city I had not spent time in, Portland, Ore. The differences were stark.

BRENT HOLIDAY, VENTURE CAPITALIST ♦

Portland and Seattle are very similar cities to Vancouver in that they are roughly 100 years old and their economic bases were resources, mining and trees. The reason that Seattle and Portland have taken off in terms of knowledge-based economies and British Columbia has not is made up of two reasons. One is that Portland and Seattle have depleted their resources by quite a bit, whereas B.C. has not. B.C. does not have the motivation, politically, to move to a knowledge-based economy when so many of its constituents are still living off the resources. In Portland and Seattle there were concerted efforts in the mid-1980s by government and industry to make the cities more technology friendly.

They increased the funding for education to get more educated people into the workforce for that particular area of technology. This concerted effort changed the face of specifically Portland and certainly Seattle. Seattle had a little bit of serendipity. They did not make as much of a concerted effort as Portland. Seattle, however, had a company like Microsoft spread out and become their anchor company. Microsoft millionaires are everywhere now. They are smart, educated in software and

36

they have loads of money. So they leave Microsoft and they start sprouting up new companies. To be a venture capitalist in Seattle is actually quite difficult because there is a lot of so-called angel money around.[i] There are numerous early-stage investors who know technology and have money to invest.

In Vancouver the anchor technology company has not arrived. There are a number of companies that are probably good candidates. Electronic Arts, for example, which is a U.S. company but has their biggest studio in Vancouver. Ballard Power Systems is a great anchor company for a technology area because fuel cells are going to change the way the world gets power, both in their cars and at their homes. A third candidate might be Creole Products, which has changed the pre-press industry in printing.

If you get an anchor company, one that has thousands of employees, and it makes millions of dollars in revenue a year, then you get a company that attracts a lot of bright minds and the infrastructure to support it. People learn about what it takes to make a successful company, and then they get a new idea and they want to start a new company. That is how the Silicon Valley initially started. Apple, Intel and Hewlett-Packard were the initial start of what became the Silicon Valley. Those are now mega-billion-dollar companies. We do not have those anchor companies here. We have $3- or $4-billion revenue companies in all of Canada, and that is just not enough of an anchor to create a Silicon Valley here.

What is Canada in terms of technology? How is it viewed in the United States? The positives are that we have an incredible publicly funded education system that has tremendous capability for research and development and is very innovative. We have great technologies coming out of the labs, government-sponsored labs, university labs, etc.

Canada has research and development tax credits. Some provinces are more aggressive than others, but the federal government has given a basis for allowing companies to do fundamental research and be

---

[i] An angel investor is usually a very rich individual who uses his or her own money to invest in businesses, looking for a higher return than he or she would get from more traditional investments. In return for their personal investment, angel investors often get highly involved in the business. Frequently this high-risk money is used as the bridge that gets a company from the self-funded stage of the business to the point when a bank or a venture capitalist would offer financing. Funding estimates vary, but usually range from $50,000 to $1.5 million.

paid back in terms of tax credits. This is very unique in comparison to the U.S.

Where it starts to fall down is that Canada lacks the managerial connections, the experience and the entrepreneurial drive. When U.S. venture capitalists talk about a Canadian company, they love the technology but wonder if the management is capable of really making it into a huge company. That is the knock against Canadian companies; they are perceived as lacking management talent as management are usually first-timers. Where do all our second-timers go? That is a good question — probably down south.

The other problem is that Canadians lack the connections. Silicon Valley executives are not smarter people. What they have, though, is an incredible connectivity, a network of people they can talk to that are customers, potential customers, potential partners, potential suppliers and potential funders of their interesting idea. In Canada we lack that connection, especially the connection to the U.S.

Over the last 30 years a lot of things have happened in Canada that have not helped the growth of a knowledge-based economy. A 22-year-old university graduate standing on the edge of a potentially huge technology career would be wary of the taxation structure and the fact that they have grown up hearing about deficits, deficit reduction and lack of competitiveness. There is almost a jaded generation of Canadians and it is worrisome that these young people, if they are interested in technology and growing technology companies, may be forced to look to the United States.

PAUL:

As I traversed the West Coast I witnessed continual frustration among the start-up, high-tech business crowd with the situation in Canada. There was a feeling of despair that innovations and jobs were skipping town. Sure, some good things were happening in Vancouver, but it seemed many people there felt it was not reaching even close to its potential. To those in the B.C. investment community, Canada's "pockets of talent" could not compete with the critical mass the United States had built, particularly in the area where a supportive business infrastructure was an immense draw to entrepreneurs looking to develop their ideas.

The major obstacle for many of these companies is growing and building beyond a certain size. Many potentially great start-up companies get "stuck" because they cannot hire (or keep) talent at their firms. Consequently, Canadian companies are being bought up by hungry U.S. firms that start to run the show and make decisions on where jobs go and what the company's future direction will be. This is fine for the owners of the company because they make a bundle selling out (although they often do not realize the true potential of their company). Furthermore, if the company moves its operations south, the local community loses jobs and Canada loses wealth.

Chris Taylor, a video-game designer and entrepreneur, was a case in point. As a truly self-made man, he did not owe the Canadian taxpayer one red cent for a university education. Chris had a high school education only, yet he became extremely successful in the U.S. video-game market. It was enlightening to discover an individual whose educational experiences differed so greatly from other individuals in his industry, yet whose profile was so similar to the other people I interviewed who were working in the U.S. Like the others, he sought opportunity and mentors.

After our initial conversation I quickly realized Chris's finest feature and skill — a passion, absolute energy and complete understanding of what he does. Chris's big success in the video-game world came in 1997 with his award-winning game "Total Annihilation." Today his company, Gas Powered Games, has grown considerably — but in Kirkland, Wash., just outside of Seattle and 10 minutes from Microsoft, not in his home, Vancouver. He now employs close to 30 young high-tech workers, many of whom he scooped out of the Vancouver talent pool.

Canada is the poorer to have lost this money-making member of suburban Seattle's high-tech elite.

CHRIS TAYLOR, VIDEO-GAME DESIGNER ✤

I run a company. We build video games. To pluralize it is an overstatement. It takes a long time to make one video game. Sometimes it takes us two years to make one. I am the chief architect of the video game. I come up with a concept, bring together a team of people and we go to work. We try to play competitive products, to see what's hot and then try to do something new. The video-game business is interesting. Every time you go to work somebody runs into your office and says, "Hey, have you heard about this, have you heard about that?" Every day is a new challenge building video games.

I started off at age 14 when a friend showed me a computer called a Commodore Pet. There was a game on it called "Dambusters" and the whole objective of this game was simply to break the dam and watch a little guy fall out. When the guy broke through the dam he said, "Help me" on the screen. My friends went into the computer code and changed "Help me" to "Oh shit!" Well, when I saw this I thought that is what video games are — being able to go in and make the computer do whatever you want.

After I got my own computer I went to Radio Shack and looked for any kind of information on how to make video games. A salesperson handed me a book on assembly-language programming. It was a total adventure trying to figure out what you needed to know because you could not go to the store and buy a book called "How to Make Video Games." I had a desire to learn so I bought every book I could, even though there were none specifically on video-game design. I would go to the stores looking for them anyway and I would talk to anybody I could.

Essentially, I graduated with only a Grade 12 education and took a job bending plastic sewer pipe. I got enough of an education bending sewer pipe to know that I did not want to continue doing that. I interviewed for a job at a company called Distinctive Software and basically they told me that I was the type of person they were looking for. They said the people with real passion typically don't have formal education. When I got my first job there at 21, I realized that I knew the least and every person I talked to could teach me something. That was exciting. I was drunk, literally, on the notion of working with those people. Those were great times. In fact, when I see people starting at Gas Powered Games that are like that, I understand where they are coming from and it's great to see. That was 11 years ago. Now I look for some kind of an education in most of the people I hire. I guess that makes me a hypocrite of sorts.

I had a choice whether I wanted to start Gas Powered Games in Canada or in the United States. In Canada, with all of the taxes and a weak dollar, it just did not make sense. Why would a person penalize himself right out of the starting gate?

There are two fundamental reasons why a person starts a company in the United States. The Canadian economy is weak, the American economy is strong. The Canadian dollar is weak, business taxes and personal taxes are high. At the end of the day it's about money.

I worked in Canada for nine years, and knowing that you would get a $10,000 bonus cheque and only receive $4,600 after taxes is the reality of living in Canada. Canada was great once upon a time for people, but it lost something along the way.

In the United States you pay low percentages — 27 percent or 30 percent or 32 percent — and your corporate tax is low. The dollar you end up with is more. When you realize that this is your chance to put something away and have a shot living a better life, you realize you are not going to get that if you stick to the grind. When you file your taxes and you send the government a big cheque, it dissolves into the system. Unless the Canadian government does something on a big scale, the individuals will just lose.

The only thing I miss about Canada is my family and my friends. I don't miss taxes, I don't miss a weak dollar. I don't miss any of that other stuff.

I would have to live five lifetimes in Canada to get to where I can in the United States. It's funny: everybody I talk to, after I tell them about what I'm doing in the States, invariably the conversation steers to, "Are you looking for someone? How can I get set up? What did you do at the border? What is the process? Who are your lawyers?" Human beings know something good when they hear about it. Frankly, it's challenging; it's a lot of work but it's worth it.

PAUL:
Interestingly enough, as Chris Taylor enjoys the perks, the low taxes, the high U.S. dollar value and does not even consider returning to Canada after a certain period of time, he still sees the Canadian border as an issue. Chris claims that most people think the Canada-U.S. border is a relatively free and porous boundary for the movement of goods and services, and to a certain extent this is true. However, when it comes to labour issues, the border is still a major concern and hassle for business owners in the United States. Despite the Canada-U.S. Free Trade Agreement and NAFTA, the border is still not even close to "free" for the movement of workers.

I heard countless stories from Nortel workers, amongst others, having to tell border officials that they were going to the U.S. for "educational seminars," not to do consulting work, even for their own company.

So there is some sort of irony in all this. Chris Taylor, who contributes mightily to the U.S. economy by creating high-paying jobs, new products for the marketplace, and increasing the U.S. tax base, still has to fight to keep his status as a resident of the United States. It made me wonder what the outflow from Canada would be if we did have a truly free border.

CHRIS TAYLOR, VIDEO-GAME DESIGNER ♣

You can get your lawyer, do your paperwork, figure out what your mechanism is going to be for coming down — a one-year visa, a five-year visa and so forth — but they have a leash on you. They are not inviting you down to live in the U.S. for the rest of your life. You go from visas to green card processes to green cards to filing for your citizenship. It is not an easy process and they definitely have the brakes on at the border.

Just because you have a business in the United States does not mean you get to live there. You could own a house, you could own property, you could build a university. It does not matter. You have to go through the processes. If your visa runs out and you cannot renew it, you go home. There is no bending of the rules, no flexibility. This is not how America started, but now there are too many people coming in and they want to stop the flow.

What I try to contribute to in the United States is the little town that our business is in. I try to be a good business in that town. I do not think on the national scale. We run a good little business, we have all our licences, everybody is well taken care of and we recycle. Those are the things I try to make sure we are responsible for. So from where I sit, I am never going back to Canada. That is my attitude. I am never going back.

The only thing I dislike about the United States is the idea that I am contributing to a system I do not fully understand. That would be the broadest sense. It is one of those feelings you get when you are driving down the street in the morning and there are thousands of cars streaming down the freeway. You think, "Well, I'm part of this system but if they do anything really stupid, I'm a Canadian," which is lame — it's probably why they want to keep me out.

Am I proud to be a Canadian? I never felt more proud to be Canadian than when I was in France and I went to Normandy. I am a World War II buff so I had to go to Normandy. I didn't have it all figured out in my mind until I drove up the beach. Every time you drive up the beach, for sometimes a quarter of a mile, half mile, you see a monument. You see the Canadian flag, the American flag, the French flag and the British flag, and you see them waving there. That was the most Canadian pride I think I have ever felt, which is bizarre because war is the wrong reason to be proud of the country. You think you can be proud of your country for the arm on the space shuttle and so forth.

That is a problem with Canada. We have to search around for something to be really proud of. Our comedians are really funny, our pop stars are really good — they are the best. We have such a low population and we produce all these really talented people. I love Canada, but not enough to live there. Not enough to live there and to live my life. No real easy way to say it, you know?

PAUL:

Although the loss of our doctors and technological talent may be deemed more serious, nowhere does the Canadian talent profile rise higher than in television and film. The list of talented Canadians who now reside and work in the U.S. is long. Dan Aykroyd, comedian, actor and writer, was one of the "stars" I spoke to about the draw of the United States. He left Canada for opportunities in New York with *Saturday Night Live* and to work in the Hollywood film industry.

It is no secret that Aykroyd became who he is today in the U.S., but he is, surprisingly, a gushing Canadian nationalist. When I interviewed him at a downtown Toronto bar, he reflected on his own "Canadianness" and on being a recent recipient of the Order of Canada.

DAN AYKROYD, ACTOR ♣

I am proud to be part of an incredibly contributive community. When I went to Government House I could not believe some of the things this group of people have done for their country. These are ordinary Canadians who give up their time to organize sports programs to help youth deal with big city pressures; they are philanthropists and achievers in science and art and music. Every one has had an international impact because of what they do for a living. Like the great Flora MacDonald, who works with refugee organizations and the abused and the suffering around the world. They are Canadians going out into the world and they make a difference. Every one of those people professes their Canadianness every day of their lives.

My father was a writer of great social policy for Trudeau, working with the Privy Council Office in Ottawa. He organized the centennial celebrations in 1967, which I was a part of and saw. My grandfather was a Royal Canadian Mounted Policeman. My mother is French Canadian and my father is English-Anglican Canadian. I was born on July 1 and raised in Ottawa and I do proudly hold a doctorate in literature, *honoris causa*, from Carleton University. I guess I have the definitive Canadian identity. I grew up in a government town and was always aware of national affairs and love that city to this day and do love my country, definitely.

Why did I leave Canada in the first place? Well, I guess I would have to turn to another expatriate, but still citizen and still devotee of the nation, Lorne Michaels. We had worked together at the Canadian Broadcasting Corporation (CBC) and he had a new concept for a live show called *Saturday Night Live*, in the tradition of live shows — Jackie Gleason, Ed Sullivan, *Colgate Comedy Hour*, Sid Caesar, Milton Berle. All the great live television comedy was produced in New York. The invitation to come to New York as a part owner in the concept was what ultimately led me to leave. I remember leaving Toronto, saying goodbye at the front door of Second City and driving my motorcycle down the New York throughway to go to work.

The decision was based on an opportunity of an extremely specific nature and that was to go back to the live, 1950s format, to write and produce and to work with Lorne Michaels, another Canadian. Paul Schaeffer was there from Thunder Bay, and Rosie Shuster, Frank Shuster's daughter, who certainly had a comic pedigree, her father being one of the great, superior comedians, as proven on his many appearances on American and Canadian television.

I had a beautiful life up here in Canada. I had the Bootleg Bar, the 505 (in Toronto), which is now famous in lore and legend. There were opportunities at CBC Radio and TV. Certainly the lifestyle in Canada is nothing like the United States. We have a purity of air and water and the way our cities are, just the foliage, the whole spirit and feeling up here is different. But to work in live television in New York with other Canadians that I trusted was the obvious move at the time.

Canadians have a rich history and many things to be proud of. We have socialized medicine. There are no handguns in the public hands. So any Canadian who does move down to the United States is going to miss the history and miss the controls we have in society.

The heart will yearn, but until certain things in the tax code are fixed so that not as much money is taken, Canada is going to lose more people. Canadians do not leave for any particular love of geophysical locations down in the United States. They go because the economic opportunities are just more attractive.

PAUL:
Yes, the heart will yearn, but will it stop Canadians from heading south and weakening our country?

In the next section I have presented the evidence I gathered in looking at how Canada's educational system plays an important role in forming the minds of our young graduates and academics. What I uncovered was a very stark profile of what is happening at campuses and technical colleges across Canada. Rarely do concepts such as paying back one's dues (subsidies for university education or technical colleges) enter into the graduate's mind when embarking on his or her career path. Not surprisingly, any sort of patriotism or loyalty to Canada pales in comparison to ambition and job opportunities. The schools know it, the aggressive new industries know it and the students know it.

Chapter III

To Educate and Vacate?

Contributors in this section:

Janice Basso   *Ben Kelly*
Noel Desautels   *Marie Klawe*
Steve Goldsmith   *Bob Miller*
Joe Goodman   *Sheila Spence*
Eve Hesselroth

PAUL:

To PROBE THE ROLE RECRUITING has on campuses across the country and how the educational system plays a role in the whole process, I spoke to job placement centres and officers across the country. All were very informative as to the pressures placed on them by industry, parents and students. The universities, once bastions of academic freedom and "pure research," have recognized that, on top of their traditional role, they must play the game of keeping relevant to the industries their students are training for.

At a convention centre called Bingemans near Waterloo, Ontario, I spent a day with our TV camera at one of the recruiting fairs created to bring graduating students and employers together. This fair was unique in that it was organized by four educational institutions in the Waterloo area and it was the largest career fair of its kind in Canada. The hosts were the University of Waterloo, the University of Guelph, Conestoga College and Wilfrid Laurier University. The fair saw over 750 employer representatives on the exhibition floor, trying to entice over 3,000 students to look at their companies. Throughout the day I witnessed literally thousands of graduates being hustled by hundreds of American and Canadian companies. I observed how the "come on down" sales pitch ranged from high salaries to low taxes in the U.S., and from extolling companies' leading-edge opportunities to championing America's better weather.

Janice Basso was one of the organizers I spoke with.

JANICE BASSO, CAREER FAIR ORGANIZER ❧

This is definitely the best employer market we have seen for university and college graduates, and so employers are competing against each other to get the best recruits for their organizations.

One of the attractive features for the employers is that they see students from the four different campuses in this particular area. Each one of those campuses has their strengths and has a particular draw with specific employers. For example, the University of Waterloo will bring in a number of high-tech employers. That is an advantage for students from the other schools; so they, too, are able to see those particular employers who might not otherwise be recruiting at their institutions.

The fair is obviously a good opportunity for students who are in their graduating year to do some networking and to try and make that match with a potential employer organization. For first- and second-year students, it is a great opportunity to come and learn what courses they should be taking as they go through their academic programs, what skills they should be developing through summer work and part-time volunteer experiences.

Employers are doing everything they possibly can to attract the best applicants. They attend career fairs, run information sessions on the campus, hold receptions and send special invitations to students to apply to their particular organization. They want to attract the best so they market as much as they possibly can.

PAUL:

Many of the U.S. recruiters were actually recent graduates from the Canadian universities sponsoring this career fair. Often only 23 or 24 years old, these newly employed graduates were sent back for an expense-paid trip to their old schools to offer enticing and enthusiastic sales pitches for the companies they now worked for. This of course allowed them to communicate on a more "one-to-one" basis with their soon-to-be-graduating peers and was very useful for American companies to ease any fears prospective employees might have about moving south.

Steve Goldsmith, a recent University of Waterloo graduate, and Eve Hesselroth recruit for Trilogy, a software company based in Austin, Tex.

EVE HESSELROTH, RECRUITER

Networking is a big part of how we recruit. At all the schools we go to we bring back the fresh alumni. They know all the students and they know programs, and so they are the best to interface with that group.

We write software solutions, mostly sales and marketing software for Fortune 500 companies. University of Waterloo students are some of the best and we hired about nine students last year. Waterloo is definitely getting a reputation within the United States as kind of the MIT of Canada and definitely attracting some of the best students.

STEVE GOLDSMITH, RECRUITER

I had other offers in Canada but I could not find a match for Trilogy. The average age is 25, and I could get responsibility and product ownership three months into the company. There, within weeks I had the kind of responsibility it would take me years to earn here. It is important because you get personal achievement and personal learning while helping your company.

Twenty people who I know from class have walked by today. At least three or four that I know would like to work at Trilogy and are individuals the company would like to hire. This system works because instead of just going to a random school and having complete strangers walk by, I actually know some of these people.

PAUL:

Clearly it was not just the recruiters who were interested in attracting the best and brightest to their companies; the students seemed surprisingly keen on presenting themselves to companies from south of the border. As the president of the Commerce Society at the University of Guelph, which represents 1,200 students, Ben Kelly summed up what was being articulated to me by students all day.

BEN KELLY, STUDENT ❧

I am a student with a background in marketing and I'm sure you are quite familiar with Microsoft's marketing efforts. Why would you not want to work for a company like that? It is important not to just limit yourself to the job descriptions in the book; you have to really go out there and be proactive and talk to corporations like Microsoft because obviously it's a tremendous opportunity.

I think a lot of these companies are looking for action-oriented people, proactive people, and I think I can fill that role for a company.

To go down to Microsoft and make $50,000 a year is the equivalent to making $75,000 up here. If I can go down to Microsoft and get the equivalent start-up amount, then basically I am increasing my salary by 50 percent. So that is obviously a consideration.

You cannot limit yourself to geographic boundaries. I must be free to go anywhere because that is something employers are looking for. They want to put their best people in the best spots. I am looking to add something to a company. I would like it to be Canadian because I am Canadian, but if a company in the States is willing to put their faith in me and they have everything I'm looking for, then I'm going to take that opportunity.

PAUL:

While I gained insight at the career fair into how companies recruit en masse for their organizations, I also wanted to examine what approach companies might have for a specific school. Harvard Business School is an excellent example of a top American institution. With its immense prestige, large corporations have aggressively sought graduates of Harvard Business School for years. I found, however, that Canadian corporations were not even on the radar screen as a presence to the Canadian graduates of the institution.

As a recruiter for Harvard Business School, Noel Desautels has seen this trend firsthand. First of all, he is part of a chain of events which takes between 25 and 30 of Canada's best and brightest out of the country per year. Noel promotes Harvard to bright, young Canadian students interested in academic challenge. As one would assume, this is not a terribly hard sell to most top students. In addition, Noel assists these academic superstars financially by linking them with grants or bursaries from former Canadian Harvard Business graduates.

The Harvard Business School Canadian alumni network has become quite concerned with another, more disturbing part of the chain. The other part of Noel Desautels's job is to help match Canadian graduates interested in returning to Canada with employers in Canada. In other words, many of the Harvard benefactors would like to see their investment pay off with these students coming back to Canada to work and contribute to the Canadian economy. While Noel maintains that the majority of students are initially interested in returning to Canada, there is evidence that numbers have steadily been on the decline, and this is becoming a serious problem.

NOEL DESAUTELS, RECRUITER, HARVARD BUSINESS SCHOOL ✤
Harvard Business School is looking for people who are top of their class academically, who are at the top of their peer group when it comes to their work experience after their undergraduate degree, and who have excelled in extracurricular activities, be that sports, military, church or community activity.

There are 25 to 30 Harvard MBA students a year from Canada. So part of my role is to pre-screen. The way I do that is I interview and get to know skills, interests, abilities, what cultural fit there would be with these 25 or 30 students per year. Once I know that, I have a better chance of matching them with the companies up in Canada that are interested in them. There is a tremendous demand. There may only be two or three or five interested in a given company, so for a company to mobilize a recruiting effort thousands of miles away in an expensive city with a chance at only a couple of people makes no sense.

Top companies from all over the world want Harvard students and are able to consistently recruit them. Hundreds of companies come on campus; it's a well-oiled machine and students are wined and dined. Companies may hold cocktail receptions on the Charles River. Students are invited out to a hotel meeting to meet the top executives of Microsoft, for example. They meet people with job offers from top companies all over the world. There is a lot of emphasis on recruiting because the people are so good; it attracts the best recruiters. The opportunities are absolutely world class and there are just not a lot of Canadian companies among the recruiters.

If I separated recruiting efforts into three five-year periods, in the last five years only 30 percent of Canadian graduates have come back.

The five years before that not quite 40 percent returned, and the five years before that it was closer to 60 percent. We have seen an ongoing reduction in the percentage of students returning to Canada who are Canadians from Harvard Business School.

The declining return rate is a great concern to some of the alumni, to the local alumni club and frankly to the school itself. The school is interested in seeing their students have a diversity of careers all around the world.

When we look at the smaller number returning to Canada, the alumni in particular are concerned. So a group of them have provided funding to help encourage the students to return to Canada. We work on finding opportunities for them and on making sure there are competitive packages of pay and of experience. Frankly speaking, what these people want is a fast track and they do not want to be given a fast track — they want to earn it.

Ideally, what a student out of Harvard Business School is looking for is really more opportunity than money, although fair compensation is appropriate. They need to be somewhat competitively compensated, but absolutely at the top of almost all the students' lists is opportunity. They want a chance to run an organization as soon as they can in their career. Things like profit-loss responsibility at a small business unit is very important to them. The chance to work with a start-up firm or a spinoff of a major Canadian firm, to work in mergers and acquisitions where they can help develop concepts and then, over time, get themselves into an operating role are all very important to the Harvard graduate. Invariably general management is the ultimate goal, where they can either have a company, buy a company, start a company or work up through the company into a general management, leadership role. These kids are hard-wired for leadership; there is absolutely no other way of putting it.

These are the people that will lead businesses, develop businesses, grow businesses in the future. If we lose them now — 10, 20 a year — think of the numbers over a period of time. What impact do 1,000 top achievers have on the Canadian economy, now or in five or 10 years?

They are Canadians and they love their country, but the reality is people get married, have children, get settled in another city and start a life for themselves. The hurdles have now increased for the individual to consider coming back to Canada. Frankly, it is a lot easier to move to

San Francisco with your company from New York than it is to move back up to Canada. It is very difficult to get them back.

The people at Harvard Business School who accept students into the school know that Canadian schools are, on average, significantly better than the average American university. The issue is Canada does not have Harvards, Oxfords and Yales. Canada has grown an excellent public education system with exceedingly high-quality standards across all universities. But what we do not have is the super elite schools, like a Harvard or an Oxford.

Perhaps Canada can move in the following direction. The Queen's University MBA is a technology MBA, charging almost full rates. Some of the top MBA schools are moving up their prices because the students coming out of these top schools can garner excellent salaries, so why not charge these young people high rates to pay for their education? If schools can pick niches, for example, if Queen's can become the world-renowned technology MBA, if the University of Toronto can become a world-renowned MBA finance school, if York University can do an international MBA where they require three languages, we could start to see some hope. Because of the public education system, it is hard to create these super elite schools over five and 10 and 20 years. Instead of forcing all schools to be all things to all people, we could have some of our top universities specialize, focus and start to attract the best professors from around the world and the best students. Success feeds on itself.

PAUL:

As you may recall from an earlier interview, Sheila Spence graduated from Harvard Business School. Her experience certainly verified what Noel Desautels said about the school, as well as confirming the profile of the kind of person attending Harvard. More importantly, she confirms the trend that Canadians graduating from Harvard are not returning the way they did even 10 years ago.

SHEILA SPENCE, BUSINESS DIRECTOR ❦

I did not see a lot of Canadian companies recruiting at Harvard Business School. I would say the exceptions were definitely that the large investment banks did actively recruit and some of the Canadian offices of big American consulting companies did actively recruit, but that was really the extent of it. I think as far as corporate Canada being there, I did not see an effort to recruit generally and certainly not to approach specific Canadians, individuals like me, to think about opportunities in Canada. This actually surprised me a little bit. I thought there would be more effort on the part of some of the larger, more prestigious Canadian companies to do that.

There were a couple of Canadians in my class who were very committed to going back to Canada. For them the most attractive positions were jobs with the investment banks or the consulting companies. From their perspective those were the jobs that paid the most, and most students graduating from Harvard have a bit of debt they have to pay off. As a group, however, most of us were not looking to go back to Canada. Would we have been more interested in going back to Canada if there were a greater solicitation effort by Canadian companies? There really was no effort to entice us and I think most people were more interested in pursuing careers in New York, particularly in my year.

This is an approximation, but there were about 27 or 30 Canadians in my Harvard Business School graduating class, and I think three or four went back to Canada. It was a pretty low ratio.

PAUL:

It did seem like a very low ratio, particularly when one takes into account that Harvard is the number-one ranked business school in the world. Nonetheless, Sheila Spence is speaking of the business world and perhaps one might expect business leaders to want to flock to the centre of the business world. But what about the academic elite, the world of professors and the institutions they work for? How is Canada stacking up?

My next stop was back to Vancouver and Seattle to do a comparative study between a Canadian university, the University of British Columbia, and an American one, the University of Washington. I hoped to examine the differences in funding, academic culture and mentality. I was able to get in contact with two hardened veterans on the frontlines of the "battle for brains," who were striving daily to make their respective schools better.

After speaking with Marie Klawe, the current dean of science at the University of British Columbia (UBC) and a former resident of the U.S., I began to appreciate the pressures Canadian universities were up against. I also visited Bob Miller, the director of technology and research at the University of Washington. He pointed out that his school was in the same game as UBC, however with a different set of tools to fight the battle for brains.

In a nutshell, I found there was immense pressure being put on universities in both countries. However, the striking problem of losing top-notch, talented professors was biting into Canada's universities to a much greater degree. In the United States a greater percentage of federal government dollars was being directed to post-secondary institutions to grow the knowledge economy. In Canada, because of our provinces' various debt/deficit situations (accumulated due to decades of either government overspending or mismanagement), money to help grow our educational institutions had either been frozen or cut. The results indicated that Canadian professors, as well as students, migrated to where better opportunities existed for research support, financial assistance or salaries. This has become a serious problem for Canadian universities, particularly in the engineering and science disciplines.

MARIE KLAWE, DEAN OF SCIENCE, UNIVERSITY OF BRITISH COLUMBIA ✤
When a faculty member chooses which university they want to work at, especially a research-intensive university like University of British Columbia or University of Toronto, they care not just about their ability to teach people but about what they are going to achieve in their research. They want to do something that will change the world. To do that they need research funding and wonderful graduate and under-graduate students. They must be able to attract technical staff to work with them, at least in areas of science and engineering.

One of the big differences between Canada and the U.S. is that in the U.S. they might be able to bring in $1 million or $2 million a year in funding. That allows them to do things in research that they cannot do with $100,000, and yet in Canada they might only be able to get $100,000. When they think about the difference they can make to the world in terms of the discoveries, they see they can do more in another country.

There is not the same level of research funding available in Canada. The federal government does not put as much funding into research and Canadian industry does not spend as much supporting research at universities.

Also, although salary is not the number-one issue for faculty when choosing their university, it does become significant when the gap is large. In some cases we have faculty members on leave to work within a

U.S. industry, and they are paid four times as much as what they receive at the university. It is very significant at this level.

Borders of countries are becoming much less important to the people who are working, particularly in the technical disciplines. Their discipline is becoming in some sense more their culture. I think that makes it hard for Canada because, traditionally, being Canadian has been something that has kept people here. And now that these borders are starting to fade, I think we could lose a lot more people.

I am literally looking at losing half of my staff in computer science in the next three or four years. And this is a department I personally built. So I am working with Simon Fraser University to try to build a co-operative faculty of multimedia and interactive learning. We need to attract enough industry, federal government and provincial funding so that we can afford to pay higher honorariums and salaries to faculty to keep them here. It is a long shot and I do not know if we will succeed.

The biggest risk factor I see in Canada is that we will lose our best young people because they see opportunities being so much greater in the United States. Not just the opportunities to get rich. The opportunities to make a difference. We can only keep the best people in Canada if we convince them that they can do as much for the world from Canada as they could across the border.

For example, I had a young woman talk to me about whether or not she should accept a faculty offer at UBC or one at Stanford or Berkley or MIT. This is somebody who would have been a wonderful person to bring back to UBC and there were lots of reasons to bring her back to Canada. In the end, I had to tell her that if what she wanted to do was to be at the top of her research field and to build that kind of career in the next five years, she should take the offer from Stanford or Berkley. The opportunities to be at the forefront of what was going on in the world were so much greater there. She turned us down and went to Stanford. The bottom line is you have to be honest with young people, you have to think about their careers, and I gave her honest advice.

It is very hard to build the kind of knowledge-based economy we want if we continue to have such high personal taxes. We cannot set our tax at a level that encourages our young people to be someplace else. We cannot refuse to acknowledge excellence and provide research support, research funding for excellence, and keep those people here. So we have to find a better balance. We have to have lower personal income tax and we have to provide better research support. And we have to be more willing to recognize excellence and to support excellence.

One of the things I love about being at UBC is we have such incredibly bright students who care about things in society. I do not think I would find that at MIT or Stanford. I do not want to lose that Canadian part of caring about human beings. We have to provide ways to allow those people to have as much impact in their technical field within Canada. If changing the definition of success means we will recognize technical excellence and we will support it, then we have to change it. If it means to stop valuing social issues and caring for people, then I would not want to change that.

PAUL:

What Marie Klawe had said resonated with some of the personal experiences I had with universities in Canada. During my three years as a student representative on the board of governors of the University of Manitoba, I had heard many of the debates regarding the role universities play in a vibrant economy and healthy society. I had also heard the mantra from many faculty members that business partnerships were becoming too much a part of the university and that the freedom of universities was in jeopardy because of this growing trend. The claim that universities would be "selling out" if industry became more involved was one I heard continually from professors in the early 1990s.

In researching for this project I began to see that Canadian universities have grudgingly become more accepting of the need to become more commercially relevant to various industries. Canadian attitudes were gradually moving toward this more American way of doing things. There was no doubt American universities accept the culture of commercializing knowledge more readily than Canadians.

Professor Klawe, with eyes wide open, sees that the university culture in Canada must change.

Meanwhile, Bob Miller understood a university's role in creating and commercializing knowledge. Bob had worked for nearly two decades at UBC and had left to take up a position at the University of Washington. He felt it was important to make deals between faculty and industry to ensure the university was given proper royalties on the knowledge it created. The University of Washington received $360 million of federal and state money for its research, $10 million from royalties and about $140 million from industry.

BOB MILLER, DIRECTOR, UNIVERSITY OF WASHINGTON
We live in truly a global economy. People will gravitate to their countries of origin but there will be tremendous diffusion across the North American borders, and people will go where the best opportunities are for developing their ideas, for developing their dreams. An American will want to do it in the United States if possible, and a Canadian will want to do it in Canada if possible, unless better opportunities are created someplace else. These people are achievement oriented, they are development oriented. They want their ideas to create something unique and valuable for themselves and for society as a whole.

The two universities are an interesting comparison because both are top-flight universities in the context of their own countries. University of British Columbia is in the top three or four universities in Canada and the University of Washington is number two. In terms of funding, the difference is that in American dollars, which is the important part of international purchasing power, UBC would probably have about $150 million whereas the University of Washington will have $600 million.

MARIA KLAWE, DEAN OF SCIENCE, UNIVERSITY OF BRITISH COLUMBIA
There is traditionally a lot more support in U.S. universities for commercialization of intellectual property and for joint initiatives between industry and universities. Over the last 10 years in Canada, there has been a lot more support in the culture for professors doing joint work with industry and starting spinoff companies. We are starting to realize that this is important to the economy, but Canada is still a long way behind the U.S in recognizing that this is a legitimate thing for universities to do.

It is important we recognize that we certainly have many other roles to play in society and in the creation of knowledge. One is to support the development of the economy, particularly in technology where it is key.

BOB MILLER, DIRECTOR, UNIVERSITY OF WASHINGTON
There always has to be a balance among fundamental research, applied research and research that can be commercialized. You can never develop a university culture, context or enterprise based only on commercial

research. The feedstock for all the research is the fundamental research supported by the federal government. Engineering schools have as their mandate doing applied research, and what we hope comes out of this in the context of an entrepreneurial spirit is commercializable research, research that has value and can be licensed to industry. It is important for the universities to learn how to manage this, to learn how to manage conflict of interest and to learn how to build enterprises. We are not going to change the cultures of our countries without changing the cultures in which our universities have operated.

The state of Washington has managed the transition to a knowledge-based economy faster than British Columbia has. There is a huge, focused environment of research dollars and expertise at the University of Washington that factors into this transition. Also, Boeing was here as an advanced manufacturing firm that spun out a bunch of other firms. There was the emergence of Microsoft as a dominant software producer and the influx of venture capital into an area that really wanted to see high-tech development move.

One of the differences is that within the United States people are going to risk failure and they are willing to finance that risk, whereas in Canada people are more averse to failure and therefore more averse to risk within knowledge-based companies, which are inherently risky ventures.

That is one of the cultural changes that has to take place both within the universities and within society. Success has to be rewarded, has to be recognized and to a certain extent success has to be lionized. When someone drives a BMW to school, somebody has to say, "I'll have one of those," instead of saying, "Who's the rich bum and how did he get that? He must have been lucky."

One of the most important changes has to come within the universities themselves. They need to embrace entrepreneurship. They have to reward entrepreneurship and to teach it. The next generation of Canadian managers cannot be risk averse. They have to be knowledgeable about high technology and embrace the future.

One of the absolute key elements about supporting the great Canadian social net is that it takes wealth to pay the bills. The next century's wealth is going to come out of knowledge creation, knowledge development and knowledge exploitation. If you do not create the wealth, you will not be able to support the great social programs that Canada has developed over the years.

The future economic support of the universities is going to come in collaborations not contributions. We have $40 million of investor research agreements at U of W a year, and $20 million in equity currently. We have $20 million of licence royalties. There are no philanthropic donations on an annual basis that come anywhere close to that. So I would argue that an enterprise model is much more important than a philanthropic model or a patronage model.

The trick is for the universities to transfer their early-stage knowledge into companies and for countries to exploit, reasonably, the knowledge capital built up at their universities. In particular, we look to starting new companies out of university-based knowledge and transferring that knowledge into the private sector through those companies.

PAUL:

What happens when one university started to find new ways of rewarding their faculties and graduate students while other schools fell behind? Marie Klawe at UBC made it clear that over the next several years, as dean of science, she would have to renegotiate expiring contracts for many of her Canadian faculty. She feared that up to half of her faculty would seek opportunities elsewhere if UBC could not offer financial offers that matched, or at least came close to matching, the salaries and research funding at other schools. She noted a particular problem with her computer science professors, people who were coveted by industry and who would have to make a decision between academia and industry.

Many stated that Canadian universities could fight this battle with the argument that the Canadian lifestyle was better than America's, or that places like Vancouver were simply nicer cities to live and bring up families in. I would agree that these arguments hold some weight, but these rebukes are becoming less cogent in today's world. I was seeing an opportunity gap that was becoming a gulf for Canadian universities.

How can Canadian universities start to fight the battle to keep our best? There are a number of factors necessary for creating a knowledge-based economy from the standpoint of transfer of information out of any university back to society as a whole. These can be summed up as follows: critical mass, intellectual properties, recognizing intellectual value, protecting intellectual value, creating business ideas and creating management that can foster those ideas. If a university could do all these, once established it would create a virtuous circle. Reinvesting money would equal more money for the school, more money for the school would equal more grants and research funding (through the government and industry), which in turn would entice more quality people to work at the university in specialized areas. This would create what people call a "critical mass."

BOB MILLER, DIRECTOR, UNIVERSITY OF WASHINGTON ▬
The first thing you need is critical mass, good faculty members who are competitive internationally and can attract research funds from federal sources, and they have to be willing to transfer that information in a way that becomes beneficial for the economy. Within the university you have to have people who know how to negotiate the deals between university professors and companies.

You need money to develop intellectual property from the university or from the federal government. Early-stage commercial knowledge that comes out of the university needs to be protected, either through patents or through copyright, and then it can be developed to be ready to be commercialized within the private sector. Next, you need managers in the private sector who recognize the opportunity and want to finance new ventures. And last, you need government policies which are consistent with a desire to get all the previous work done.

The future economies of North America are going to be dependent on our ability to create, develop and exploit knowledge for the public good. We are not going to be able to depend on inexpensive manufacturing in the future. Other countries can beat us with low wages and good manufacturing. We are not necessarily going to be able to compete in the commodity-based economies the way we used to. The future is going to be in developing technology which makes us competitive against low-wage markets.

Canada has a particular problem because qualified people will likely move into the United States unless there is a receptive community for them. The trick is to allow these people to take a leave of absence, develop their ideas commercially within a start-up company and then be able to move back into the university. This allows the faculty members to develop their intellectual property and receive rewards for it, and when they come back into the university, they bring brand-new operating procedures and knowledge from the private sector.

PAUL:
When I made my trip down to Silicon Valley, and in particular to Stanford University in Palo Alto, Calif., I saw what "critical mass" really was. The link between the burgeoning information and technology industrial sector and Stanford was incredible. I spoke to Joe Goodman, a 40-year veteran of Stanford's engineering faculty, and he definitely supported what University of Washington's Bob Miller was making a case for.

JOE GOODMAN, professor, Stanford University 🇺🇸
Stanford University will typically grant a two-year leave of absence without pay to a faculty member to participate in a start-up company. We have to do that in moderation because someone has to be here to teach the classes, of course, but it has been done many times. The experience of participating right from the very beginning through a successful initial public offering is an experience that they bring back to campus. It really instills enthusiasm and their teaching is relevant for the students' future development. It is the right attitude for Stanford to have.

We do it within the bounds of certain constraints that govern conflict of interest and conflict of commitment. When the individual comes back, we want to be absolutely sure that Stanford is the top commitment that this individual has and that in no way is their work at Stanford in some sense biased by their financial interests in the outside companies.

BOB MILLER, director, University of Washington 🇺🇸
The whole process of commercializing intellectual property out of the university is barely 10 to 15 years old. We are all running experiments. We have to be careful to protect our home institutions. What is important is a very open communication among the faculty, among the administration and among our industrial partners. As we move forward we need to make sure that our communications are very good.

Canada has invested as much, if not more, than any other industrial nation in higher education, and Canada has to rise to the challenge of taking advantage of that in developing their economy of the 21st century. There has been investment, there has been achievement, and now you have to take it to the second stage.

No one has a better education system than Canada. That is the heart of a knowledge-based economy. They have to now develop management and develop financial wherewithal to capitalize on that investment.

JOE GOODMAN, PROFESSOR, STANFORD UNIVERSITY ▦

When I came to Stanford in 1958 as a graduate student, the university had a reputation for being a very good Californian university, particularly in the undergraduate population, which catered to the children of wealthy Californian families. Over time that has changed dramatically. It is now recognized as a university of international strength.

Silicon Valley has grown up around Stanford. In 1958 one did not have to go very far to the south to find apricot orchards. Those orchards are almost all gone now, and as you travel south you will travel through the heartland of the industrial base of Silicon Valley — Intel, Cisco Systems, Sun Microsystems, all of the big companies. The Valley has increased dramatically the number of technical people that live here. The population density is higher, the cost of housing has risen tremendously, making it difficult to import people to Silicon Valley from the rest of the world, but we still manage to do it.

Would Silicon Valley exist without Stanford? I think it would not exist in its current form without Stanford. Many people attribute the founding of Hewlett-Packard to be the beginning of Silicon Valley. Stanford played a role in that. The head of the department of electrical engineering actually loaned money to Hewlett and Packard to help them start the company. So in that sense perhaps nothing would have happened with respect to Hewlett and Packard without Stanford.

Stanford serves as a magnet to draw talent to the area. Without Stanford, the growth of Silicon Valley would have occurred at a much slower pace and it would not be the premier place for the electronics industry. A symbiotic relationship has developed where Stanford helps Silicon Valley develop, but Silicon Valley helps draw talent to Stanford as well. So both parties benefit.

I think the most important thing Stanford does is act as a magnet for bright people, particularly young people who come to get an education and find this area so attractive they end up staying. We feed a lot of such young people to industry in this area and, as a consequence, that keeps the machine going.

We feel that our interaction with industry strengthens the courses we offer, makes them more relevant, and as a consequence the university has devised a multitude of ways to interact with industry. The Stanford Center for Professional Development is a television network that broadcasts live many of our engineering courses to local industry in the Bay area. Local companies find this an attraction that helps them hire employees because they can get a graduate degree basically from their company's location.

Stanford has a very positive attitude toward technology licensing. When professors have a patentable invention, the university will patent that invention and will share the royalties between the university and the faculty member, and will license this intellectual property to companies, either local or not local, on very reasonable terms. This is a very positive way we interact. Basically, the university will hold a patent for an invention by a Stanford faculty member or even a student. The university will market that patent and try to find companies that are interested in licensing the patent. They will collect licensing fees or royalties and will then distribute those fees to the faculty member's department, to the faculty member himself or herself, and in this way the ideas that are generated here are easily spread through the Valley and beyond.

We also have many centres that have industrial members who contribute financing to help support the beginnings of new research projects. These help make our research relevant and help us initiate research projects that we could not otherwise do.

Stanford has benefited enormously as successful entrepreneurs generously give back to the university. A few years ago Stanford instituted a new fund drive to raise $200 million in endowment to support fellowships in the sciences and engineering for graduate students, in an attempt to reduce our dependence on federal funding for graduate students. This fundraising effort has been very successful. The university has raised $140 million of the $200 million from people in Silicon Valley. This kind of philanthropy really allows the university to do things that it would not otherwise be able to do.

A couple of young students came to me when I first became chairman of electrical engineering some years ago. These two graduate students in electrical engineering had developed a database that was on the Internet. They developed it entirely in their spare time using Stanford computers, and they had reached the point where it was growing in both popularity and equipment needs and they wished to take it off campus. The question to me was, "Would I waive any Stanford rights to what they had developed?" They needed my approval as well as the approval of several other people within Stanford. Since it was developed in their spare time and in a very incidental way using Stanford equipment, we decided the best policy was to waive any rights to what they had created. They went off campus, and this became Yahoo.

Yahoo was really born at Stanford, created by the two young graduate students. The attitude of not needing to claim rights of ownership in this creation paid off for Stanford in the long run because the two students who created Yahoo have given back to Stanford several million dollars as gifts. The university, in the long run, has benefited enormously from their success.

CHAPTER IV

SMALL NUMBERS — BIG PROBLEM:
THE OPPORTUNITY COSTS FOR CANADA

Contributors in this section:

Laurie Baggio	*Bob Miller*
Jim Burns	*Harris Miller*
Noel Desautels	*Jack Mintz*
Don Devoretz	*David Pritchard*
Brent Holiday	*Paul Swinwood*

PAUL:

ONE MAY ASK WHY I chose to build the structure of this book the way I have so far. And it is a good question. It is my belief that without a background of knowledge and a context to build upon, the "brain drain" (a widely used term) of people moving south is simply just another story about people leaving and doing things elsewhere. But what does it tell you about the country? What may it say about any deep-rooted dysfunction in Canadian political practices over the past 30 years? Most importantly, what does it tell us about the allegiances of Canadian citizens, when these people recognize our country's relative decline with respect to our southern neighbour?

To draw conclusions from what I was hearing thus far was certainly not a difficult task. In listening and discussing the various issues presented, it was clear to me that at least part of the economic strength of a country's future depends on its ability to successfully nurture, develop and market a knowledge-based economy. I think it is fair to say that Canada is not reaching the heights it could in this regard.

All of us in Canada of course know this country is blessed with an abundance of commodities and natural resources, however, it made me wonder if our reliance on those same resources has slowed our move, both economically and politically, to the new economy? Is Canada playing on the old playing field? Perhaps the trickling departure of Canada's highly skilled and educated citizens is a symptom of these people looking for a new and more dynamic field.

My next step was to explore what was "pushing" people out of Canada or "pulling" them south. The next section is an analysis of what I heard from people about the real cost of lost opportunities to Canada in a newly global world of workers and companies.

PAUL SWINWOOD, SOFTWARE HUMAN RESOURCE COUNCIL ✦
What Canadians have to understand is that, as a global economy, the ability to work, the ability to be employed, the ability to find challenging jobs will go where the opportunity is. Borders, artificial nation borders, artificial financial borders, do not exist in the world of information technology, nor do they exist in the world of the knowledge-based economy. The ability of a person or the ability of a company or the ability of a corporation to work anywhere in the world is something that our standard institutions, like governments and corporations, are having to address on a daily basis.

JIM BURNS, CHAIRMAN, GREAT WEST LIFE CO. ✦
Effectively, the world that the current young generation knows about is the world of free trade and globalization. They do not know anything different so it would be much more difficult for them to understand the importance of having a border and protecting Canadian culture. I suspect if you did a poll of 20-year-olds in Canada, they would have difficulty trying to understand why there is such a furor about protecting Canadian magazines, for example. If Canadian magazines are any good, they should do well. If they are not good, they won't make it, regardless of whether American magazines hold some control over our magazines or not.

BOB MILLER, DIRECTOR, UNIVERSITY OF WASHINGTON ▆
Human resources, in particular knowledge workers, are what will develop the economies of the next century. Those are the people that are absolutely critical for generating and maintaining the wealth of a country.

Look at the high-tech community within Seattle, which is billions of dollars of sales, independent of Microsoft and independent of Boeing, that hinges on a few hundred senior executives and thousands of important knowledge workers. All of them matter, they all add up.

A critical factor is who they are and what skills they bring. If only 100 key managers come to the United States from Canada, and they start 100 new companies that are successful, that would be 100 important companies that Canada would not have developing there. A small number of people can be very important.

PAUL SWINWOOD, SOFTWARE HUMAN RESOURCE COUNCIL ✤
We work in a global economy in the high-tech community. The challenge and the opportunity to work for the best organizations in the world is what motivates people. What we need to do in Canada is make our companies be perceived as the best companies in the world to work for.

Currently we are not doing a good job of getting that message out. Between our tax levels and the perception of taxation, our inability to reinvest, the ability to invest and then have it taxed away has caused the perception that Canada is not the best spot to be.

The effect of losing our best and our brightest is definitely a cost to the Canadian economy and a cost to Canadian reinvestment. At the present time no one has a solution as to how to stop it.

PAUL:
What was being implied here was just how important a few players in the economy can be to a country. When these people make the choice to head south, we incur what is called an "opportunity cost." It may sound complicated, but it really isn't. Opportunity costs simply refer to the potential benefit that would have accrued to Canada if a highly valued person did not leave with his or her talents. Really it is the "potential" that Canada forfeits when a choice is made by someone to leave.

Jim Burns, a heavyweight in Canada's business community, has witnessed the tug of America on the people in his company. He illustrated opportunity costs in a way anyone can understand.

JIM BURNS, CHAIRMAN, GREAT WEST LIFE CO. ✤
It is not a cost that one would see on a balance sheet or a chequebook. It is what "might have been." It is the difference between what happened

and what might have happened. Had that educated and highly subsidized dentist or doctor stayed in Canada, over a lifetime he would have, amongst other things, probably paid millions of dollars of tax. Society would have easily recaptured the cost of educating him and so on. If he leaves, it never shows up in the government's books, but the fact remains that the opportunity for gaining is gone and you never get it back. The cost of that is tremendous.

NOEL DESAUTELS, RECRUITER, HARVARD BUSINESS SCHOOL ✤
It may only be five or 10 a year who have graduated from Harvard who are not coming back that we would like to see back, but multiply that over 10 years. It is fairly clear that the calibre of highly qualified people matter to Canada. Think about that in terms of the jobs that they would create. Think of that in terms of the organizations that they would lead and the companies they would start. It really does matter to get these people back to Canada.

For example, out of my 80 classmates at Harvard, one became the CEO of the largest hotel chain in the world, another was the CFO of Disney Corporation before 30 and another has been made the secretary general of the United States army. These are just three out of my 80. These are people who go out and make a difference in society, and the Canadians that go to Harvard often become highly successful.

There was another really hard-charging young fellow who has now started up an e-commerce business. We would have loved to have him back to start that company in Canada, but the funding sources were in Boston. It is difficult to get people like that to come back, and it is a real loss because if we can create opportunities in Canada — in Vancouver, in Toronto and Montreal — we can really do something for the Canadian economy.

DON DEVORETZ, PROFESSOR, SIMON FRASER UNIVERSITY ✤
The main concern is that the number of young people who are leaving will not come back if they establish themselves in the United States. The Prime Minister's Office, the advisory board on skills recently heard my testimony saying that a lot of countries like Ireland, China, India, Germany and now Canada want to find out how to get their nationals back from the United States. I told them that if they are young, married, with children and a mortgage, there is likely nothing Canada can do to entice them back.

PAUL:

What Don Devoretz was saying was in fact a problem I bumped into continually during my travels and interviews across the U.S. What I heard from the hundreds of people I spoke to was that once somebody makes that initial choice to live and work in the U.S., the odds of getting him or her to come back to Canada become much more difficult over time.

Time and again I heard stories of young graduates who were supposedly in the U.S. for less than two years say, "I'm just down here for a couple of years. I will make some money, pay off my student loans with American dollars and come back and establish my career in Canada." Nice story, but there was a catch. The closer these former Canadians came to the two-year mark of living and working in the U.S., the less assured they were in their convictions to come back to Canada. Like clockwork, after two years, with their new lives well established, the statements began to shift. I began hearing stories more like this: "Well, I always thought I would go back, but now I have such an enormous amount of responsibility at my job, a fantastic social network of friends (many ex-Canadians themselves), good pay and a topnotch company health-care plan. I just can't see myself going back for a while. Did I mention the weather? Oh, I like that too. But don't get me wrong, I still love Canada."

As Sheila Spence said, "When I moved to New York, it was because I was graduating from college and I was looking for something fun and exciting to do. No, I would never have imagined eight years ago when I moved here that I would still be here."

This is no exaggeration. I assure you that my two-year theory will stand up to any challenge.

The problem with this troubling trend, of course, is the threat Canada faces of losing all those potentially important people and opportunities. I began to look at these people as "the vital few," as one economist once referred to the people who leave.

Clearly, everyone who moves to the U.S. is not going to become the superstar of the U.S. economy, but these people are "vital" for one reason: as a demographic group, they are the most talented and entrepreneurial people in society, so the odds that they will make a difference is very high. It only takes one Michael Dell or Bill Gates to move the world; these are the people who can move markets and create the net gains for all of us, but if they leave, everybody's value in Canada goes down.

How many of these people are heading south? Again, the number of people going south is less relevant than the quality, but the trends do seem troubling.

DON DEVORETZ, PROFESSOR, SIMON FRASER UNIVERSITY ✤
There are two things about the numbers — there are permanent and temporary movers to the U.S. The permanent movers are going up slowly, the temporary movers are exploding because of the NAFTA agreement. They went from zero to 60,000 in the last 10 years. Admittedly these are temporary visas, but we estimate about 20,000 people have converted to permanent residents out of those 60,000.

A temporary visa creates a "back door" into the United States. This was intended to be a one-year-or-less visa for Canadians travelling there to work when NAFTA was set up. However, our findings indicate that people are going there for one year or less, and then looking for further employment to convert to full-time status in the United States. For now, only one in three are using this back-door route to get into the U.S. Nevertheless, when word gets out that this process is so easy — that you can convert to a permanent status right at the border — then I suggest the numbers will go from 60,000 visas to easily 120,000 visas.

In 1999 the number of people that left in a highly trained field for the United States alone was equivalent of the output of two and a half Simon Fraser universities. That seems to be very suspicious, that we should be running two and a half universities for the United States. As long as the job machine in the United States keeps churning out demand for new workers, you will see a continued flow of Canadians draining to the south.

PAUL SWINWOOD, SOFTWARE HUMAN RESOURCE COUNCIL ✤
What the Software Human Resource Council has found from the companies we have surveyed is the people Canada is losing are probably the most experienced, the brightest, the ones who have the most to offer small high-tech companies in Canada. They are being lured away to the U.S. because the U.S. has a shortage of between 300,000 and 400,000 people with exactly those skills.

The numbers we have been shown quantify the number of people going out of Canada versus the number of people coming in. What has not been captured is the quality and the experience and the knowledge level of those two groups. Anecdotally, we are seeing much higher numbers of the senior people leaving and junior people coming in.

Canada is definitely feeling the negative effects of the skills shortage in the United States.

DON DEVORETZ, PROFESSOR, SIMON FRASER UNIVERSITY ♣
That we are losing people to the U.S. is extremely costly because it's highly selective. The United States has put in immigration legislation and we have signed legislation under NAFTA which purposely creams the crop. The brains that we're sending are the best of the best. You must not confuse numbers and quality. This is a high-quality group leaving — small numbers, big problem.

PAUL:
The demand for highly educated and skilled workers was growing so quickly in the U.S. during the late 1990s that the U.S. government was forced to respond to the pressures being placed on it by the industry players most affected.

The U.S. is a fairly protectionist country when it comes to its views of immigrants flooding into the country. However, what I witnessed was an intense political lobby to increase the numbers of people the U.S. would allow into the country. The reason was simple: many of the high-tech companies, and the universities as well, were incredibly strapped in their ability to hire quality people. Senator Spencer Abraham, a Republican from Michigan, grabbed hold of the issue and successfully swayed public opinion and the U.S. Congress to see the benefits of changing the law to allow 50,000 more skilled labourers into the United States per year. The law that came into effect in early 1999 will see the U.S.'s high-tech immigration numbers increase from 65,000 foreigners to 115,000.

The effects have been predictable for Canada. With the U.S. accepting more people into the country, there is a greater chance they will look north of the 49th parallel to find them. Our language and popular cultures are so interconnected with those of the U.S., it would be hard to imagine that we wouldn't be the first place U.S. companies would look for educated workers. Furthermore, what I discovered was that many of the people heading south were not simply university graduates. Many were Canadians with years of experience and skills.

In the U.S. I perceived a political system that was very much in tune with the needs and changes in the economy. When they noticed that their economy was in trouble, the political system engaged and acted. A public debate over the new economy ensued within Congress on both sides of the political fence, both Democrat and Republican reacting to the situation.

Meanwhile, back in Canada the needs of the new economy, the issues of labour mobility and the brain drain simply seemed to inflame entrenched political interests. In political terms the brain drain became either a right-wing, tax-cutting conspiracy, or a call to arms from the left wing that the brain drain didn't exist. Sure, a few questions about the issue were placed in Question Period of our House of Commons, but nothing happened.

To illustrate this point, I can recall a frustrating part of my research phase for the TV documentary. Back in 1999 I made numerous calls into our federal government's bureaucracy to see what kind of government response the brain drain was receiving. In searching for potential on-camera interview subjects, I was in pursuit of senior people in our government to comment upon whether the movement of highly skilled workers to the U.S. was seen as a serious problem or not. I was able to get in contact with numerous senior civil servants in the industry and immigration ministries. These were all very helpful people who actually had done quite a bit of work on the issue. All the people I spoke with (they asked that I not use their names) were very concerned with the trends Canada was facing in terms of our talented labour heading south. These civil servants also sent me numerous documents outlining their policy work in the area — all of it pointed to the fact that Canada was slipping economically vis-à-vis the U.S., particularly in the area of worker productivity.

I was not surprised by the information these civil servants were providing because I, too, was coming to the same conclusions in my research. What surprised me was the inability and reluctance of these learned bureaucrats to stand up and state even one word about the issue. Not one person on the inside of government would publicly admit that the brain drain was a matter of concern, or even potentially a matter of concern. Why? Because, of course, Prime Minister Chrétien's stated policy was that the brain drain was a "myth" (front page, *Ottawa Citizen*, June 11, 1999). John Manley, his industry minister, mused that it might be a problem but became strangely silent on the issue after one public utterance to that effect. One would not want to cross the boss, as they say, and actually speak the truth. No, it seemed better that the government spend the nation's hard-earned tax dollars conducting all this productivity and brain-drain research in the upper echelons of our federal civil service, then have the research put on a shelf to collect dust.

It was no wonder our political system creaked along as usual and continues to, denying that there "might" be a problem.

To see the stark difference between our political system and that of the U.S., I spoke with several people involved with this political lobby to increase the flow of these highly skilled workers into the U.S. I have outlined what David Pritchard, the director of recruiting for Microsoft, said to me. He was a man who was clearly feeling the pinch of the tight labour market in the U.S.

In Arlington, Va., I also spoke with Harris Miller, the president of the Information and Technology Association of America. His job was to politically represent the interests of the largest high-tech firms in America, such as Intel, Microsoft and Hewlett-Packard, to politically push their agendas of freeing up the labour market.

DAVID PRITCHARD, DIRECTOR OF RECRUITING, MICROSOFT
I think Microsoft is typically pictured as a company that goes after hiring people right out of college and that is the majority of our people. In fact, less than about 20 percent of our people are recent college graduates. More are people that have anywhere from two to 15 years' computer software experience. So although we do want to increase our hiring out of colleges and universities, it's still a minority compared to the rest of the hiring we do.

There is a war on talent out there. A recent study from a national trade association projected that there are close to 400,000 open job positions in the high-tech area in the United States and Canada. This is the competition Microsoft is up against. A lot of companies are hiring technical people, all the way from General Motors to companies like Microsoft, Intel, Hewlett-Packard, small start-ups and so forth. All are looking for the same type of people to put together programs for their companies.

So we do look for people wherever we can find them and sometimes that means we do find a lot of those people outside of the United States. But we don't necessarily go looking for them outside the United States; they sometimes come looking for us.

HARRIS MILLER, PRESIDENT, IT ASSOCIATION OF AMERICA ▆
We are very supportive of a relatively open immigration policy to the United States for the fundamental reason that we are part of a global economy. So the legislation that Senator Abraham (Republican, Mich.) introduced that we backed so strongly, that was passed and signed into law, substantially increased the number of skilled workers who can come in. However, we still do not believe it is the solution to the information technology workforce shortage in the United States.

The real solution has to be in educating and training Americans.

DAVID PRITCHARD, DIRECTOR OF RECRUITING, MICROSOFT ▆
As much as we talk about free trade agreements, getting people and goods across the border can sometimes be a challenge, either direction. To help this situation, Microsoft was part of the initiative to raise the visa cap — the quota of people coming into the United States — with a lot of support from firms in Silicon Valley, Intel, Hewlett-Packard, Cypress Software, a number of firms as well as universities that are trying to attract great talent in the United States. Given the labour shortages that we have in the high-tech area, finding people has been a big problem for us. And so working with Senator Abraham and the U.S. Congress and Senate, we were able to get the visa cap raised. Thus far it has been very beneficial to a number of companies along with Microsoft.

PAUL:
Canada is a free society with a relatively open border, and most people would agree that immigration to Canada is a blessing for this country. I think that the public in general believes that Canada should maintain our pluralistic society by allowing immigrants to continue to land on our shores and aid our workforce.

But what about the fact that we educate Canadian students with huge subsidies, up to 80 percent or even 90 percent of their post-secondary education in some cases like dentistry and some areas of medicine, and then they leave the country?

Some would argue, "No problem, we will just get immigrants to fill those positions." It is a nice proposition, however, what I found was that there are what economists call "churning costs" to the economy when we try to replace a Canadian educated within our school systems with a non-Canadian immigrating to the country. The costs are not the same as when a Canadian leaves.

DON DEVORETZ, PROFESSOR, SIMON FRASER UNIVERSITY ❧
The free exchange of highly skilled people is a very contentious debate. Nobody wants to stop that. It has improved the economy in Canada and the U.S. However, we need to level the playing field.

When we lose someone from the Canadian economy who has been trained by the Canadian taxpayer, we lose the taxpayer subsidy, which is between $100,000 and $200,000 for each engineer who leaves. The Canadian taxpayer metaphorically sends that money to Bill Gates. That is one part of the churning costs. If we try and replace that person from the rest of the world, there are added costs. First of all, there are costs of recruitment, finding this person, language training, bringing the family in, etc., which is about $60,000. The simple one for one movement implies about $160,000 to $200,000 in churning costs.

The Canadians who are leaving have been trained in a First World economy with one of the best educational systems in the world. They know the culture of the United States and Canada, but most of all, they speak English and have access to the latest technology. Canada is trying to replace them with people who do not speak English, who need to be retrained and who also suffer from discrimination in the labour market.

It is not a simple one-for-one exchange because every person leaving costs between $100,000 and $150,000 to the taxpayer in subsidies and another $60,000 to $100,000 to absorb a replacement. That is in the neighbourhood of $200,000 to $250,000 to the Canadian taxpayer. It would be better to keep these people than try to replace them. None of that cost would be absorbed by the Canadian economy.

The next question is the quality difference — can you really substitute a scientist leaving University of British Columbia with an immigrant scientist from a foreign university? We doubt it and how we check this is we look at the productivity of these workers.

The average productivity of workers who are highly skilled, who have entered from Third World countries to Canada, has fallen dramatically. They are not a replacement for those who are leaving and so we have a problem here. How many foreign graduates does it take to replace a UBC graduate? Well, it looks like it is going to take a large number, much larger than the number that are coming in.

We can also take it from the Canadian point of view. We send highly skilled people from Simon Fraser University to Redmond, Wash. We then go to Shanghai, China, to recruit replacements. If you stop for a moment and think about the ethics of this, it is the Chinese peasant who is subsidizing Bill Gates. That truly is morally bankrupt.

PAUL:

What Don Devoretz states here is the paradox of the brain drain. On the one hand, the instinctual argument can be made that by sending our tax-subsidized, educated brains south of the border, Canada loses completely. They take their education and Canadians see no return on their investment. However, on the other side of the argument is the case that the movement of our best people benefits Canada because these people gain skills, contacts and expertise from the U.S.'s talent pool, and they then bring their skills home and build companies here — a "brain circulation" as opposed to a "brain drain."

Well, which is right? Certainly we must raise a couple of issues first.

Clearly, any movement of skilled humans and talent benefits both countries. By increasing wealth and human capital, by having the best people in any field creating new products and innovations in any one place, the world economy gets stronger. Consequently, if more jobs are created (demanded) in certain industries and all surplus labour (unemployment) is sopped up, then we all benefit. In theory, if that Canadian who heads south does gain skills and expertise and then turns around and brings them home, this should not cause detriment to one country at the expense of the other. It must follow, then, that if that same person never comes back, although the world economy (and U.S. economy in particular) is strengthened, Canada's is surely weakened relative to the nation that receives our educated Canadian.

With that said, it made me wonder about the reciprocal agreement we university and college graduates have with our government. If we don't pay for our real cost of education, and almost all of us do not, shouldn't we Canadians be forced to "pay back the government" if we leave the country without paying back into the system with our taxes?

DON DEVORETZ, professor, Simon Fraser University ♣
Large numbers of people are leaving. We tracked the 1994 graduating class of nurses all across Canada. Forty-two percent of them now work in the United States. Why were so many people getting nursing training in the mid-1990s when Ontario, British Columbia and Quebec were shutting down hospitals? Are nursing students stupid? Did they not know that jobs were not going to be there? Of course not. They knew that jobs were not going to be there, but they also knew they could move to Texas. That is the kind of moral bankruptcy we have to watch out for. If we charged them the full cost for their education and they left for Texas, fine. But we didn't.

Let us convert it over values. How much do you owe when you leave Canada when the numbers indicate the cost to the Canadian taxpayer is about $200,000 to $250,000 for each highly trained person to leave? Canada has about 20 really good universities. We are not in a position to add two more to service the high-tech companies in the United States. The total for the last 10 to 12 years is approximately $15 billion of taxpayer subsidy handed over to the United States. This is money we could have used to generate jobs or increase high-tech research in this country. We should think twice about whether we want to keep this uneven playing field where the subsidy makes the table slant to the south.

Australia had a problem with students leaving and not paying their loans. Students traditionally do not pay their loans. What they instituted was a loan, and whether you had to pay back the loan was contingent on whether you stayed in Australia or not (i.e., if you leave, you pay), and that's what I'm suggesting. If a student receives an education in Canada and receives 80¢ on the dollar from the taxpayer, the student does not have to pay the government subsidy back directly if he or she works in Canada. It can be paid back over the years through taxes. However, if the individual takes a high-paying, $200,000-a-year job in the United States, then they should pay back the full cost of their education. How can we do this? When students go into engineering schools, they should have to sign a contract. At present, MBA students at Queen's are paying the full shot. So we can either make them pay the full shot or ask them to pay when they leave. How enforceable are these contracts? Lawyers in the U.S. will enforce them in two minutes by going to court. It's not a problem.

We could also offer a tax deferral. Why not entice that graduate from Waterloo back by saying, "Three years with Bill Gates, you come home, you stay here for three years, we'll give you a break on federal taxes." Reverse subsidies are the carrot of my scheme but the stick is, if you do not return, you have to pay us. The combination of the two would definitely stop the brain drain.

PAUL:

So that is the debate. Should students pay the full load for their education, or should they be forced to pay back their subsidy if they leave? Surely the discussion of the rights and responsibilities of students who get an education in Canada cannot be done justice in this book, but it is one that our education system in Canada must grapple with in the future.

Although Don Devoretz was coming up with some fairly interesting ways of having heavily subsidized students repay the Canadian taxpayer for their education, this seemed off base. On the one hand, most people in Canada I interviewed were saying we need to fuel our universities and colleges with more money to educate more Canadians, while on the other, that we should charge the hell out of them if they make a rational choice to leave the country. It is a nice argument, but it seemed that we should probably focus less on the education side of things and more on dealing with the reasons people leave.

Not surprisingly, the tax system and the fact people were being "pushed" out of Canada due to our country's taxation rates was a recurring theme. One of the most respected people I spoke with on this matter was Jack Mintz, a highly regarded University of Toronto business professor who was hired for a two-year term with the Department of Finance in Ottawa. He was commissioned to do an in-depth analysis of Canada's tax system and specifically its business tax system. If anyone could shed some light on Canada's tax system, he was the guy.

JACK MINTZ, PROFESSOR, UNIVERSITY OF TORONTO ✤
In terms of the tax system, what influences whether a person migrates between Canada and the United States are the total taxes paid by an individual relative to their income or the average tax rate, not the marginal tax rate which people sometimes quote, which is the additional tax that you pay when you earn an extra dollar of income. That is a totally

different calculation. In Canada we have relatively high marginal tax rates at relatively low levels of income, unlike the United States and many other countries.

We define a wealthy person in Canada as an individual who earns approximately $80,000 (Canadian). In the United States they define a wealthy person at about $140,000 (American) or $200,000 (Canadian). In other words, we define rich people at relatively low levels of income. As a result, when an individual achieves income levels that are in the $60,000 to $80,000 range, our taxes are actually quite high relative to our income, even if we take into account expenditures made in Canada on health care and education. The United States still provides a fair amount of support through the education system for graduates, and many businesses will provide health care to their employees. Once you actually do the calculations, Canada has to offer about 20 percent more in salary just to compensate for differences between the benefits and taxes that are paid in Canada compared to the United States.

Therefore, if a business wants to locate in Canada and attract these kinds of individuals, they have to be prepared to pay more salary income to an individual in order to have that person work in Canada. If they move the production facility to the United States, they would be able to pay about 10 percent to 15 percent less to some of these individuals. This has been very important to the high-tech industry and a number of other industries that do require more skilled workers to work in their business.

DON DEVORETZ, PROFESSOR, SIMON FRASER UNIVERSITY ✤
In economic terms, the push factors from Canada include lack of job opportunities, low wages or high taxes. The pull factors to the United States are its close proximity, low tax rates and career opportunities. For example, when students from the University of Waterloo engineering department leave to go to Redmond, Wash., they always cite the pull, the fact that they are going to have long-term career opportunities. Very few of them mention the fact that it is difficult to find a job in Canada. Whether one is being pushed or pulled depends on their occupation. It is also a combination of forces. The NAFTA agreement and changes in the U.S. immigration act have made it much easier for Canadians to be either pushed or pulled to the United States.

There are three things that indicate there will be an increase in Canadians moving to the U.S. Firstly, taxing people at a very high rate will send them scooting. Secondly, when firms move to the United States because of a lower tax environment, they take people with them, creating more jobs. So this is a downward cycle in Canada. The fact that both the firms and the individuals are attracted to the United States doubles the effort. Finally, the information technology and high-tech industry is exploding in the United States, turning that country into an incredible job machine. Unless Canada can keep Nortel and smaller companies here, students will continue to leave.

PAUL SWINWOOD, SOFTWARE HUMAN RESOURCE COUNCIL ❧
The people who are going are the ones who are not being challenged in their current companies, in their current positions, or perceive that they have no opportunity for advancement. Part of the studies that have been done have shown that salary is only number six in the reasons why people move. Other reasons include lack of satisfaction, recognition, opportunity, as well as retraining and re-education.

JACK MINTZ, PROFESSOR, UNIVERSITY OF TORONTO ❧
Canada first must reduce its personal income tax levels, especially for the upper-middle-income group of skilled workers, in order to maintain an attraction for individuals to stay in Canada and for businesses to locate here and be willing to compensate people in a fair way. Secondly, the government should make major changes to the business tax structure, particularly, take away the discrimination of tax policies against service sectors, our knowledge-based economy. This is the part that is now becoming very internationally competitive and Canada is losing jobs to other countries. We have to have a business tax structure with much lower rates of tax and a broader basis.

Finally, the government should look at the employment insurance system and think about linking the actual contributions those firms make to employment insurance, and link those contributions to the actual layoff experience of the firms. That might actually induce many firms to reduce the turnover that they impose on workers by laying them off in order to collect employment insurance benefits during the layoff period.

When people decide to leave, they may leave for many reasons, including getting better compensation abroad. But once you factor in the higher level of taxes in Canada, then the brain drain is part of a tax revolt for those people who leave. We must do a great deal in this country in order to bring tax levels down just simply to reduce the brain drain and to encourage people to stay at home and take advantage of opportunities that we have here.

PAUL:
The brain drain as a tax revolt? An interesting notion, and the more I reflected on Mintz's comment, the more I agreed with him. However, from my interviews, I would note that taxes are not the first thing on people's minds when they decide to start a business or take a job elsewhere.

Early on it became clear to me that everyone, young and old, responds in a very rational but personal way to his or her political and economic circumstances. Young people in particular make decisions based on a variety of reasons but are clearly the most mobile in society. They don't yet have the roots, homes, families, nor the responsibilities or biases of the older, more staid Canadian crowd. Clearly, taxes and what governments do with those taxes once they collect them were affecting these people — if they recognized the fact or not.

How the tax system and political system affected the growth of companies was also something I noted. What I was hearing was that the biggest difficulty Canadian companies faced was growing their businesses from the five- and 10-person company to the 50-person company. Investment capital, the ability to mentor and finding the time to recruit qualified people were just a few of the challenges small companies were up against. These "Canadian" challenges were costing us all.

JACK MINTZ, PROFESSOR, UNIVERSITY OF TORONTO ♣
Canadian businesses are facing a serious problem in that they face much higher levels of taxation, especially in the service sectors. These are our knowledge-based sectors of the economy, such as business services, communications, wholesale trade and transportation. The levels of taxation in Canada on these businesses are much higher than what you would find in the United States and in many of the European countries. That raises a number of very important issues because if you look at the brain drain you can't just look at the personal tax side, you must look at the business tax side since that can influence how many jobs are created in Canada.

Growth industries in the future are going to be in the service sectors, and high levels of taxation make it harder for these industries to grow as fast as they could. Therefore, we do not get as many jobs in these sectors as we could if we had a better business tax structure. The level of business taxation in Canada has impacted on investment made by Canadian companies as well as foreign companies in Canada. High tax levels on the business side have reduced the amount of investment and labour creation.

BRENT HOLIDAY, VENTURE CAPITALIST ❧

Having mentioned taxes, and having mentioned all of the issues that have faced Canadians over the last 30 years, it is interesting that our government, specifically the federal and provincial governments, are in a push-me, pull-you kind of situation. On one hand, they are subsidizing research and development for growth. Their Technology Partnerships Program is giving tons of money to the aerospace industry, like Bombardier, etc. They are putting a lot of money in education and fostering this growth and talking about the knowledge economy.

On the other hand, they are taxing us to death. It is really difficult to understand how the government is putting these two things together into a cohesive strategy for growing what will be the dominant economy for Canada. We are always going to have resources. We are blessed with that. The problem is that it's not going to be the industry that my kids are going to grow up and take part in. They will be part of a knowledge economy.

JACK MINTZ, PROFESSOR, UNIVERSITY OF TORONTO ❧

In Canada there are two types of special relief given to businesses. One type is given to the old, traditional industries, which has basically kept them around longer than perhaps they should be, or has certainly allowed them to exist in a bigger form than they should be at this point. That is one type of distortion. The other type of distortion is that governments tend to like doing a lot of selective tax decreases for businesses, and yet the actual experience with these special credits is that they are not all that successful in generating the kind of activity that we expect.

What is very important is that a business is able to adapt new technologies. We do not have a system that tries to make sure that the tax system does not get in the way of adaptation of technologies. In fact, we have a tax system that currently imposes a very high penalty on businesses that tend to become more efficient and obtain profits because they have to pay such high tax rates on those profits.

LAURIE BAGGIO, ENTREPRENEUR ✤
Unfortunately, governments in Canada tend to react extremely slowly to these situations. We need to change our priorities. Instead of giving $250 million to save a pulp and paper mill (like to the Skeena pulp mill in B.C., which is currently in receivership), we need to focus energy into following the new technologies. If we don't, Canada is going to lose what is probably the most important juncture right now in terms of where we are going. Canada cannot rely on being dragged along by the goodwill of what is happening in the United States and their push into technology.

If our talented people are pulled to the States and if their companies are acquired and then their key personnel are slowly pulled to the States, Canada loses that critical mass, that networked gel that creates new knowledge and new opportunities. Canada loses tax dollars and the ability to build a whole infrastructure. Canada will basically lose the war economically.

JACK MINTZ, PROFESSOR, UNIVERSITY OF TORONTO ✤
When businesses pay high taxes, it actually can be a silent killer of jobs. For example, Ireland in the past 20 years has had tremendous growth, and the way they did it was not by reducing personal taxes. They did it by reducing business taxes. That attracted a lot of multinationals to Ireland who wanted to use Ireland as a base to move into the rest of Europe. The Irish have been very successful strategically in attracting these businesses, and now Irish per capita income is higher than the United Kingdom. This is a complete reversal over the experience of the past 100 years. In fact, Ireland once had a brain drain to the United Kingdom and now there is a brain drain going from the United Kingdom to Ireland.

The United States is Canada's most important trading partner, with 80 percent of our exports going to the United States and 20 percent to the rest of the world. Clearly, we have to have our eye on the United States but remember that businesses are looking at North America as a region. It becomes a question of where that business should locate when coming into the North American region, in terms of their production facilities. Whether it's a Japanese company or a German company, they will look at Mexico, Canada and the United States and evaluate the advantages they get from each of the three different countries.

One of the things that Canada could do much better than the United States is on the business tax side. We could offer an environment for businesses that could attract them to come here because we have a good skilled labour force and we have a number of other advantages as a country. The one area that we are actually penalizing businesses on, compared to the United States, is the tax system. We should not only match the United States, but do better to make Canada attractive for businesses to come here first.

This would have a tremendous effect on the brain drain because if you create jobs and opportunities in Canada, people will not want to move down to the United States. It is not enough to educate the work-force and have things like health care provided for.

PAUL:

Jack Mintz hit on a touchy issue here. Canadians love to boast about the generosity of their welfare state and how it makes Canada a much better place in which to live. And there is no doubt that many Canadians are proud of many of our government's legacies in this regard. However, the problem is that Canada's generous employment insurance or even its medicare system is simply not of interest to Canada's highly educated youths.

The reason people leave is because they are offered more enticing, career-enriching offers elsewhere. When young professionals are weigh-ing the pros and cons of staying or going, the social safety net in Canada is not even on their radar screens. Yet the taxes that are taken from them to pay for the social safety net are high on the priority list. The truth is, most young, highly skilled graduates who head south of the border do not worry about their health-care needs because the companies they are going to work for cover these incidentals. They merely go with a signed contract in hand.

Surely we, as a nation, must find the balance between what our gov-ernment takes from us in taxes and how it spends that money with the needs of fostering more competitive companies and keeping the people who work for those companies in Canada.

JACK MINTZ, PROFESSOR, UNIVERSITY OF TORONTO ✤
Governments have an important role in society. They spend money on programs. They regulate the economy and it requires resources to do these things. The taxes we pay actually help support the government expenditures that are made. Sometimes governments do things that make the economy worse rather than better in terms of both its public expenditures, and if they are wasteful, people end up paying excessive rates of taxes.

PAUL SWINWOOD, SOFTWARE HUMAN RESOURCE COUNCIL ✤
Part of what we have not done in Canada is recognize what we get for what we pay. We have a high level of taxation. We also have a high level of services, relatively speaking, compared to some other countries. We are taxed significantly higher than Americans. What we have to do is figure out whether that is a good thing or a bad thing and how to marginalize the difference or change the differences. We must look at things that encourage Canadian companies to reinvest so it makes Canada and their company a better spot to work.

JACK MINTZ, PROFESSOR, UNIVERSITY OF TORONTO ✤
The breaking point that makes a nation or its government want to change comes when the public realizes that something must change. If Canadians realize that we have been falling behind the United States over the past 10 years, that we have had an increasing gap between personal income in the United States and Canada, they would start saying, "Gee, there's something wrong; we're not doing the right thing. There's some problem in what we're achieving." A recession where we end up increasing unemployment will force the government to address that. People will point at what factors may have caused those problems and, of course, there are a number of problems now. So the fact that Canada has a per capita income now that is significantly less than the United States and has dropped several thousand dollars below the U.S. compared to where we were a number of years ago, on a per capita basis, is a telling sign that something needs to be fixed in this country.

PAUL SWINWOOD, SOFTWARE HUMAN RESOURCE COUNCIL ✤
So any time wasted in not making the right decisions and support decisions will affect us in our ability to grow. There is an opportunity

cost. The opportunity that we are missing out on is to become a bigger player in the world economy rather than maintaining the percentage that we have.

CHAPTER V

AGENTS OF CHANGE:
CAN CANADA BE A WINNER IN THE GLOBAL SWEEPSTAKES?

Contributors in this section:

	Bob Miller
David J. Blumberg	*Harris Miller*
Noel Desautels	*Jack Mintz*
Joe Goodman	*Paul Swinwood*
Brent Holiday	*Peter Wolken*

PAUL:

HOW WILL CANADA DEFINE ITSELF within North America and the world in its attempt to be a winner in the 21st century? In this final section, I have tried to pull together interviews of the various people who have seen Canada as a bastion of economic possibilities, but also a place that has squandered much of its potential.

After traversing the various "meccas" of where talented Canadians flock and where business booms, I began to notice numerous similarities between these places. Although some of the similarities have already been presented in this book, this final chapter draws the details out to a greater degree.

This section is called "Agents of Change" because the term came up several times during my travels and interviews, in reference to entrepreneurs. These "agents" are the risk takers in our societies who make things happen and change the world with their ideas or businesses. They have been nurtured, partly by luck as well as by economic circumstances, to ensure that the U.S. will always be near the forefront of innovation, as well as near the top of the world's economic ladder.

While travelling the economic growth areas of the U.S., one cannot fail to see that their economy is riddled with investors and venture capitalists willing to back new people and enterprise. This fuelling of enterprise, as well as the U.S.'s relatively free economy, allows the creative (and sometimes destructive) power of new ideas to develop or crash, but eventually allows them to commercialize. Money alone cannot bring a vision to fruition. The entrepreneur needs the human element as well — value-added investors, marketing and distributing partners — a critical mass of talented individuals who help ideas and products materialize.

One of the most eye-opening experiences I ever had was my trip to Silicon Valley, where the attitudes and openness of the people was so strikingly different from those in Canada. There I had one of the finest interviews during my entire journey, with 30-something David Blumberg, who operated his venture capital firm in San Francisco. As a former resident of Canada, David had witnessed and observed Canadian business culture for a number of years. He opened my eyes to the world of financing and what it takes for new economies to grow.

DAVID J. BLUMBERG, *VENTURE CAPITALIST*

The reasons that Silicon Valley has grown and developed and continues to increase its production output and productivity of entrepreneurial companies are several fold. The most important is human capital. We also have the requirement for financial capital that is going to take the risk to invest in early-stage ventures. Early-stage venture investing is a risky business. The majority of companies that are started fail. Sad but true. But those that go on to succeed really build most of the new job growth and a lot of the wealth that is driving the economy of the United States forward. So we need to have the kind of investors who are willing to take a calculated risk. These are not gambler investors; these are investors who do their homework and understand specific markets, whether it is Internet or semiconductors or biotechnology.

You have this coalition of human capital, intellectual property, financial capital, all in a very beautiful, temperate climate. Underneath it all there is a base structure of appropriate economic and physical infrastructure that the United States is blessed with. We have a relatively low capital gains tax rate; we have relatively moderate taxes compared with

Canada or some European countries. We have a very strong physical infrastructure, airports, highways, all of that. Most important, the telecommunications infrastructure needs to be very strong.

JACK MINTZ, PROFESSOR, UNIVERSITY OF TORONTO ♦

Capital gains tax is applied to the income a person gets from selling assets. You pay a tax on the difference between the price that you sell the asset at and the original cost that you purchased the asset. The difference is what is referred to as a capital gain and you can pay a 25 percent tax rate on the difference in the selling price and the original cost of the asset. That, effectively, is what a capital gains tax is. Generally, most capital gains are earned by wealthier individuals in society, and people have often talked about the unfairness of cutting capital gains taxes as a general policy because it will mainly help the very rich rather than being a broader-based tax cut to all parts of society.

There is an argument underlying that, although we have to remember there is a tremendous amount of risk capital that goes into investments, and the capital gains tax, while it does take away the gains from an individual, it really shares the losses and so it penalizes risk.

DAVID J. BLUMBERG, VENTURE CAPITALIST 🟦

Mecca is the centre of anything. In Silicon Valley, one can make that metaphor ring very true because we are constantly being visited by clients from overseas, from Israel, from Australia, from Sweden, and from companies based on the other coast, the East Coast, the New York and Boston and Washington area. They must come to the mecca of the 21st century to do their business deals, to find the venture capital, the calculated risk investors that we specialize in working with, and to make the business deals that are going to make their product a market leader from here — and then out to the rest of the world.

Maybe a better analogy is that California, specifically San Francisco, was the home of the 1849 gold rush. Thousands of people came to California in a period of just a few months after news of gold finding was announced to the rest of the world. In a few short years San Francisco sprung from nothing to a metropolis and many fortunes were made. Most fortunes were made, frankly, by people in other businesses, not the gold-mining business itself. The people who sold the Levi's jeans and the pots and pans and so on. Now in Silicon Valley there are many services and businesses that provide support to all the entrepreneurs. The Silicon Valley boom of the 1990s will far surpass the value in absolute inflation-adjusted terms of anything like what was made in the physical gold rush of 1849. So this is truly a gold rush, and it is a gold rush that will benefit the entire world.

PETER WOLKEN, VENTURE CAPITALIST 🇺🇸

These companies are built not so much on infrastructure, not so much because everyone came to mecca. They are built on a vision of the entrepreneur and an idea that can make use of the infrastructure of the Internet, and that is a worldwide network that everyone in the world has access to. All they need is a low-cost personal computer and a connection to the Internet.

Entrepreneurs can start companies spread more widely than the concentration of a mecca, of a Silicon Valley. The Internet is a culmination of something now that will give a lot of people opportunities to create businesses and create wealth.

DAVID J. BLUMBERG, VENTURE CAPITALIST 🇺🇸

The structural forces that have propelled risk taking and encourage it and reward it are fairly easy to understand, and they include, for example, a lower capital gains rate. Capital gains tax is tax on investment income or risk-taking income. It is not salary income. For example, if I build a company, invest in the company, grow the company, sell the company for more money, that is considered a capital gain.

If you are a wage earner who is taxed at a certain tax rate in a very prestigious company, it may be very attractive to stay. To leave a big company like Bell Canada or Bank of Montreal takes away prestige and adds financial risk. To go off and risk all to take a start-up position for a company that you can grow and then sell, and your gains will be taxed at the exact same rate as you would be as a wage earner, is a very rational thing to avoid. The government is hereby encouraging you to stay with the status quo and be a wage earner for the rest of your life.

On the other hand, if you have a reduced capital gains tax, an incentive for taking risk and starting a new company, selling it and keeping more of what you have produced, then the rational person will be more inclined to take that risk and start a new company. The United States has a better capital gains structure than Canada. We also allow entrepreneurs to reward their employees with stock options. Often the crucial negotiating issue is not salary, it is equity in the start-up — a piece of the company and that potential to let it grow. Those kinds of dynamics cause the risk factor to be socially very acceptable.

BRENT HOLIDAY, VENTURE CAPITALIST ♣

When you work for a number of years in a technology start-up and eventually go public, you have poured your life into this company. You have worked hard to make sure that the company can be successful, and at the end of the day your reward is not only the experience you had and the salary you made, but the chance that, as an individual who helped create this wealth, you will get a piece of it.

When this happens in the United States (the capital gains tax being lower than in Canada), the options these people receive make them instant millionaires in many cases. These people turn around, start a new company, pour most of the money back into the new company and create a whole new opportunity for other people to make money. It increases employment and the infrastructure keeps getting bigger because people reinvest in the economy. That is the argument for capital gains that is compelling. You have to reduce capital gains tax on individuals in Canada so that they may take that wealth and go and do more things with it. They can reinvest it in new technologies, in new companies, and that is what helps the whole thing grow.

BOB MILLER, DIRECTOR, UNIVERSITY OF WASHINGTON ▄

One of the important differences between Canada and the United States has to do with the remuneration for young managers of start-up companies. Within the United States options on stock and equity positions in companies are a key element of how they become rewarded. The Canadian system and the American system are slightly different, but what is really different is the huge tax that you pay on income in Canada, so that a very successful manager gets taxed at a very high level. If Canada finds it unacceptable to change income tax levels, then in order to become competitive, it has to make a major change in the way it handles stock options and equity positions. In other words, there has to be a real reward for these young people to sacrifice so much of their lives to build these ventures.

The number of people that you have to provide incentives for within the high-tech community is small and what you want to do is reward the winners. It will only be a few people who drive major developments.

PAUL:

In regards to the dynamism of the U.S. economy, I witnessed that a troubling trend was occurring between Canada and the United States in terms of job creation.

During the late 1990s the U.S. economy nearly doubled Canada's in terms of job creation. Since that time America's unemployment levels have significantly (and consistently) been lower than Canada's, at times reaching half our jobless rate. This means that, even when Canada closes the jobless gap for short periods of time, the demand for labour in the U.S. is much tighter. The U.S. job-creating machine throughout the late 1990s did have negative effects on Canada — not in an absolute sense, but in a relative one. Yes, the growth of the U.S. economy meant that some of their surplus capacity and work was being exported to companies in Canada. But is this a good thing or bad thing? Some would state that this is fine for Canadians and we certainly benefited.

However, what I observed was that Canadians in many industries were simply becoming the low-wage workers of the U.S.'s fast-growing companies. With our weakened Canadian dollar, American companies could pay salaries for 62¢ on the dollar and get equally talented and hard-working employees if they set up an office in Canada. Plus, if they were in the right industry, they could often get some nice federal government research and development tax credits to boot.

Now jobs are jobs and many Canadians might say any jobs are better than no jobs. But let's look a little deeper. When a company sets up shop here, are we not, in a sense, being used as "slave labour," a country able to sell our wares cheap because of a diluted dollar? Are we fostering industries based on a weakness, our cheap dollar, instead of a strength, our brains? Further, who is calling the shots in these business transactions? It was clear it was increasingly becoming Americans with little or no allegiance to this country. Sure, they may look at their company's bottom line and see Canada as a good place to do business (we speak English and understand their culture), but their ties here were often weak.

This was a trend I saw across the board with highly skilled employees in Canada, and these employees were not oblivious to the situation.

They were the same employees who were demanding to work for the American arms of their companies and get paid in U.S. dollars.

As a Canadian, it made me consider if this is what we wanted to be as a nation — comparatively advantaged over the U.S. because we can do a lot of their businesses' grunt work at a cheap rate. Perhaps I am being harsh here, but it forced the issue and made me think about what we must do to change our situation.

I wanted to know what the cultural attitudes that played into the U.S.'s success were. Was their business culture fostered from the political structures they have, or was it some sort of genetic entrepreneurial trait? Some people are indeed "born" to be risk takers, no matter where they happen to live. Perhaps the people on the margin, those potential risk takers who might be willing to take a gamble on starting a new company were being cultivated in the U.S. yet hampered in Canada. Or maybe there was simply something in the Canadian psyche holding us back.

Here is what I found.

DAVID J. BLUMBERG, VENTURE CAPITALIST

There is a difference in the acceptance of failure that I have seen in Canada, in Japan, in Australia and other places versus the United States. Here failure is not a loss unless you have not learned anything from the failure. In other words, failure is something that teaches you on the path to greater understanding.

For example, in Silicon Valley entrepreneurs will often start an introduction or an autobiography about themselves by talking about their failures. They talk specifically about what they learned. There may be some embellishment along the way, but as long as there is insight and introspection gained, it is not seen on a résumé as something to be shied away from or embarrassed about or to cause a block in a career path. On the contrary, it really can be seen as something that is character forming and sort of a crucial steppingstone to a higher and better career.

Acceptance of failure has a lot to do with acceptance and understanding of risk. Structural forces drive cultures far more than we like to admit. We think that we are all very different and unique cultures, and that is true, but brainpower is relatively equally distributed around the world. I have met geniuses in Canada and Japan and Israel and Australia. They are not all in Silicon Valley. I have also met a lot of entrepreneurial people in those countries. I have also met a lot of people with the opposite characteristics, who will never take any risk, and people who are not particularly bright.

Therefore, you cannot say that California and Silicon Valley succeed because they are all inherently culturally risky or brilliant. It is just not true.

BRENT HOLIDAY, VENTURE CAPITALIST ❧

In Canada you have the psyche of a fear of failure. I cannot illustrate this any better than my personal experience of going to Silicon Valley with one contact, two open days and an objective to talk to a group of people in the venture capital community and the technology industry about a specific company.

I had two full days of meetings because everybody had another contact for me to speak with. When I went to Toronto to do the same thing, it was a closed shop. They do not trust you upon meeting you for the first time enough to risk that you might not turn out so well if you are referred to a friend. You have to take the risks even in just introducing people. It is all about connectivity, connections and networks. You have to meet people, you have to talk to them and you have to introduce them to other people. It is serendipitous and that is what they understand in the Silicon Valley. If I introduce you to a source of funding, then somewhere down the line you are going to come back and help me. Canadians do not want to take that step because, if they fail, they are done. We really have to change that.

Are Canadians like that because we have had this culture throughout time? I don't think so. We had a lot of great entrepreneurs in our early history. Is it because of the tax structure over the last 30 years? Or the fact that we stand on the border of the 49th parallel and watch the Americans in all their bravado, and we like to make fun of them? There is something that Canadians are just missing in terms of willing to take that step and say it doesn't matter. If I succeed, great; if I fail, so what? I start again. When you talk to American venture capitalists about entrepreneurs that have failed, they want to hear what they learned, what went wrong and why they won't make that mistake again.

Certainly if you are a serial failure, then people will start to look at you differently. However, one or two black marks on your record should not affect your ability to go out and start again and raise money again

94

because you should have learned from that experience and know what to do this time.

In the United States there is a complete lack of the fear of failure. It is "the glass half empty" or "the glass half full" attitude. If American entrepreneurs try to start a technology company and it does not work, they start another one or work for another company. There is no contingency plan for failure. The idea is to go hard and grow a company and make it successful. That starts in the public school system and it is called the American dream.

DAVID J. BLUMBERG, VENTURE CAPITALIST

Entrepreneurs are a very unique phenomenon. Entrepreneurs are people who see things that do not exist to the rest of the world. They take calculated risks that most other people would not attempt. Being around people like that is very motivating and very rewarding. The reason I think entrepreneurs are so important to a country is that they tap a country's own potential.

Canadians are very well educated, charming, erudite, bilingual people in general, and that is a great advantage in this world. You have it all on your doorstep and the sad thing is, if you let the Americans take all of the entrepreneurs away, you will be doing only yourselves a disservice. The entrepreneur will still flourish but he will flourish on American tax rolls, not on Canadian. He will flourish far away from his family and create his family in America. The point is that Canada can absolutely compete with America on many scores — lifestyle, convenience, community — Canadians have a great deal to be proud of. But you must respect and reward your entrepreneurs, men and women, Protestant, Jewish, Catholic, Muslim, Buddhist, white, black, yellow, green — it does not matter.

Entrepreneurs are important because they create the new jobs of a society. The corner grocery store, founded by immigrants generally, in a few generations becomes a giant grocery chain. These are the kind of people that start with nothing and are compelled to start something on their own. Out of this necessity comes the invention of entrepreneurship. If you then reward them and let them keep a good portion of their returns, they reinvest and they build new shopping centres or companies or buildings and employ more people.

Countries have to reward change and they have to embrace change, not resist it. Entrepreneurs are the change agents of society in the economic sense. One of the lessons that Silicon Valley has started to teach the rest of the world is that the time scale of change is shortening. Decisions, events, processes are happening faster than they did even a decade ago. You need entrepreneurs because they can react quickly to fast-changing events. Large corporations tend to react more slowly and sometimes governments react the slowest of all. So if you want to have a country, society, that embraces change (and with change comes growth and economic development and prosperity), you have to let the entrepreneurs lead.

BRENT HOLIDAY, VENTURE CAPITALIST ❦

In Canada we have an interesting paradox in that we are an educated society, a wired society, and we like to think of ourselves as extremely progressive in building a knowledge economy. The government and industry are doing a lot of things toward that end in terms of giving us a great educational institution. We are getting a lot of innovation and research and development from universities that are creating technologies that could be huge technology companies. The problem is we still have the baggage of the resource economy. We have what stifles the knowledge economy, which is the lack of forward thinking when it comes to funding, the lack of forward thinking when it comes to building out an infrastructure that supports this and the real lack of forward thinking when it comes to what it takes to keep smart people growing this industry in Canada.

If you cannot compete on taxes with the immediate neighbour to the south, or on the issues of supporting an entrepreneur to grow a company, then you run into a problem in Canada where the economy will not grow as quickly as it could.

Entrepreneurs are risk takers by definition but there is this tremendous fear of what happens if it fails. That permeates everything that this entrepreneur is going to do in Canada. When it comes to trying to find money, the pitch is almost apologetic.

In the United States they walk in, they sit down and they say, "I'm going to be the biggest company in this particular technology that has ever been." They are probably wrong, but if you start out with that attitude, you are going to develop a company along those lines. You are going to mobilize the troops, people are going to get excited and you are going to start something.

In terms of creating an entrepreneurial culture in Canada, there are two arguments one can make. Firstly, high taxes, the large national debt and the structural things that have been put in place over the last 30 years make it tough to be an entrepreneur in Canada. Secondly, what really is the issue comes down to the Canadian psyche when it relates to risk taking and as it relates to entrepreneurs.

PAUL:

Although I believe the interviews are clearly telling the story here, it is worth noting that there was one insight I don't think we as Canadians can ignore anymore. That is the compounding effect of economically falling behind other nations in the world.

Canada's standard of living is still high, but as most Canadians recognize, it did not rise at all in the 1990s and has increased only marginally since then. We have been slipping, no matter what our political leaders try to tell us.

As has been presented throughout this book, it is starkly clear that the structures Canada has built over the last 30 years in our economy, through government taxes, business practices and regulations, have all contributed to Canada becoming a less entrepreneurial culture than it might otherwise be.

The threat is there, the question is — are we up to the task of changing things before we fall further behind?

DAVID J. BLUMBERG, VENTURE CAPITALIST 🇺🇸

In many respects Canada may have a better lifestyle in certain ways than the United States. In the past Canada has benefited from a lot of dependence on natural resources. Those natural resources are not going to be the wealth of the 21st century. Canada has to change its rules because the structure of the game is changing. America has already leapt ahead in that realm. America has transitioned primarily by deregulating a lot of industries, telecommunications, transportation and banking. All of this deregulation and the move toward free trade have made America a very competitive, in the good sense, robust economy that is open to the world. It is this competitiveness and openness to change that continually reward America.

The issue about an economy growing has to be considered both in an absolute sense and also in a relative sense. The information economy is growing at such a rapid pace that if you are not running with it, you are falling further behind in the skill set and the mix of capital and intellectual property. The know-how that the U.S. is building up is going to be harder and harder to attain from a second position. All of Silicon Valley and most economists and entrepreneurs would argue the same thing — trying to eke more and more out of Mother Nature by cutting down more trees or mining more coal or diamond or gold is not going to make it in the 21st century.

We are living in a world where ideas are far more valuable than diamonds. Ideas are far more valuable than corn, and what we need to do is grow ideas and reward those ideas. Everybody can have an idea regardless of what colour or race, religion or anything they are. Canadians have great ideas, and what I think the point the Canadian entrepreneur would make is, "Let us be Canadian entrepreneurs and flourish inside our own boundaries."

Everybody is important in an economy, in a society. The argument that says that if one or two percent of the entrepreneurs leave a country, it will have no effect because we still have the remaining 98 or 99 percent is not a very holistic argument. If you take the lions out of the Serengeti Plain, what would happen to the ecosystem? There are only a few lions and there are thousands of gazelles and zebras and antelopes and so on. But you absolutely need the balance there and the lions play a critical role as the top carnivore. I am not saying that entrepreneurs are carnivores, but they play a role in generating jobs that is probably on a numeric term quite equivalent.

JOE GOODMAN, PROFESSOR, STANFORD UNIVERSITY
Why are the entrepreneurs, that one or two percent of the population, so important to the economy in general? It is because they are individuals who believe that they can take an idea and turn it into a company. This is a tremendous challenge. The idea has to be good, of course, but the execution of that whole process is filled with pitfalls, and the entrepreneurs who succeed are exceedingly talented individuals because they had the ideas and they turned them into a profitable company and made money for the shareholders as well.

DAVID J. BLUMBERG, VENTURE CAPITALIST
The entrepreneurs take calculated risks, they leave their jobs at the big institutions, they risk misery and starvation for a while, and then they hit it big and build a big company, which ends up employing thousands.

America still has protectionist elements in society, especially in the political establishment, that resist the kind of change they see. However, by and large America has been very receptive to change and it rewards people for it, and ultimately ends up benefiting the whole society.

Canada is a more conservative society that is less competitive in its nature. There are, for example, a few large supermarket chains in Canada that dominate retail commerce. There are a few large banks in Canada. There used to be only one large telephone company. The size of your economy dictates that there might be fewer players than in America, but the ultimate good of the economy will come when you have a robust and competitive marketplace, not a closed shop of the old boys' network. That is the big difference between Canada and the United States.

Canada has all the basic compounds, culturally speaking, to be a flourishing entrepreneurial society. Canadians are very well educated; there is a strong work ethic; there is a general feeling of trust and a tolerance that pervades Canadian society, which is the hallmark not only of today but of the culture of the 21st century. The problem with Canada is that it does not reward entrepreneurial risk taking. It does not reward capital. Unfortunately, a lot of people think there is a tension between free speech and cultural expression and free capital. That does not have to be the case. You travel around the streets right outside our offices here in San Francisco and you will find people who by day are building software products and working on building billion-dollar companies and by night are wearing purple hair and running around at the dance clubs.

There can be a great synergy between free spirit and free enterprise, and I do not think Canada has to retreat into a fear that an open economy will cause people to lose their rights or somehow float down on the human rights scale.

BRENT HOLIDAY, VENTURE CAPITALIST ❧

I have seen small thinking a lot in entrepreneurs in Canada. Their business plans come in with projections for a $5-million company in five years, which is not a big company. One must think big in order to be big. In general, Canadian entrepreneurs are a little hesitant to say that they are going to be a massive company.

The creation of a small-thinking culture is probably a product of the last 30 years, of taxes going up, unemployment staying high, deficits, etc. Where Canadians want to take baby steps, Americans want to take the huge step. Let the venture capitalists and other people that are assessing your opportunity be the realists. You be the dreamer and the opportunist as the entrepreneur and have the other people bring you back down to earth. Otherwise you will not be big.

There is a lot of small thinking going on from the financier's side as well. It is not enough to say you are a risk-capital provider, you really have to think like a risk-capital provider. You have to be a risk-taking person, just like an entrepreneur. The entire community of financial providers needs to rethink what risk really is here.

For example, in venture capital it has been said that if you invest in 10 companies and one is a huge success, all the others could fail and your entire fund will still be a success. That is exactly the American attitude toward venture capital. Benchmark Capital in the U.S. consisted of five individuals with an average age of 31. They invested $6 million over a year in eBay. At its top, that $6 million was worth $3 billion. They could have taken all of the other 30 investments they made in their fund and driven them into the ground, and all of the people that backed them would be ecstatic because they have a $1-billion gain on their $6-million investment.

In Canada we want to make sure that at least three or four of our 10 make $10 million or $15 million or $20 million so that our fund can be successful. A lot of venture capitalists in Canada will say the Canadian companies have not shown the ability to grow to the heights of an eBay. Hopefully that will change as people realize you need to embrace the U.S. and make sure that your company is known and has connections in the U.S. so you can get those U.S.-style valuations in your company.

HARRIS MILLER, PRESIDENT, IT ASSOCIATION OF AMERICA Borders are not irrelevant, nation states are not going to go away, but the need for global co-operation is increasing dramatically. The need to break down traditional barriers in the economic arena such as tariffs, such as so-called non-tariff barriers, such as the movement of highly skilled people being relatively easy, such as a commitment to recognize each other's laws. Those kinds of barriers have to come down. We are not going to have one world. I think people who talk about that being a part of the digital economy are really dreaming things that are never going to happen. I do think every government has an obligation to understand that unless they are part of the effort to bring down these barriers, then they are going to lag behind. Because they are going to find they cannot participate in the global economy if they are not willing to contribute to bringing those barriers down.

NOEL DESAUTELS, RECRUITER, HARVARD BUSINESS SCHOOL ❧
Americans value more the business, the person who creates the business, the person who starts a company. While we in Canada, of course, have created some great enterprises, have lots of entrepreneurs, it just does not seem the same. It really feels that there is a lot more entrepreneurial spirit in the United States.

If I were to sum up what I thought we could do in Canada, it might just be a cultural change, greater acceptance of business, greater interest in the entrepreneurial spirit, greater acceptance of leadership and that the people who are the highest chargers and the greatest achievers of society actually contribute a lot. Perhaps some of them got there because they really did accomplish a lot and grow businesses and build businesses.

PAUL SWINWOOD, SOFTWARE HUMAN RESOURCE COUNCIL ❧
In the United States they have recognized that the knowledge-based economy will be the next major global mastery, and that, as we go into the 21st century knowledge-based economy, is what is going to drive most governments, most technologies and most economies. The information technology sector, which is a knowledge-based economy, will be the next area of global importance. At one time it was agriculture, at another time it was the early manufacturing age. Today we are in the global knowledge-based economy. And the United States of America has said they will be the dominant sector or dominant society in that sector.

DAVID J. BLUMBERG, VENTURE CAPITALIST ▥
One needs to have the right intellectual capital, the right kinds of patents and proprietary ideas that are unique, the right management and the right kind of investors at the right time frame. One needs to have the right type of labour agreements and the right type of contractual agreements with partners. All of these coalesce to make something a success or a failure.

PETER WOLKEN, VENTURE CAPITALIST
It is a lot more important to think about what can go right than what can go wrong. It is very easy to find lots of people to point out things that can go wrong. It takes leadership, entrepreneurial spirit and just plain guts to start a company, and a lot of hard work. There are a lot of things that can go right. To point back to the early days of Apple Computer when Steve Jobs and Steve Wosniak were basically kids that started that company and did not know it could not be done — but they did it. So that has to be the focus. There are a lot of obstacles to building a successful company. It takes passion, perseverance, persuasion and a little luck. Maybe some capital helps.

I know Canada can do it.

PAUL:

And so the question for we Canadians is, how can we make the grass as green as possible on our side of the border? Well, I hope this book has plowed some of the groundwork in looking at what faces Canada and what impedes our country as we strive to create a more vibrant economy.

What I have tried to present here is that the brain drain is simply a warning shot, a wake-up call for the rest of us that something troubling is occurring in Canada, and that the people at the top of the economic ladder tend to react to it first.

Of all that I heard in my travels, one quote made by David Blumberg in San Francisco stood out as embodying what I want to say in this book.

DAVID J. BLUMBERG, VENTURE CAPITALIST
So if a few percent leave, and they are the entrepreneurial percent, or the scientific elite, or the entertainment elite, or the athletic elite, or the best lawyers or the best doctors, what happens to the rest of society? The rest of society is poorer for it.

So if your entrepreneurs in Canada continue to migrate south to make their dreams come true instead of remaining in Winnipeg, Vancouver, Toronto, Chicoutimi, and using their entrepreneurial skills at home, then Canada's going to be the poorer. America's going to be the beneficiary, but it's going to happen whether you like it or not.

EPILOGUE

HENCE, THAT IS THE CHALLENGE — we know the world is going to move ahead whether we like it or not, so are we going to be poorer for it or will Canada change? Are we going to let the Americans (and others) steal the economic show, or will we try to surpass them? Let us hope for an optimistic response.

I could sum up here by suggesting all is going to be fine, that Canada will do just fine. However, I cannot. I admit that I am not too optimistic about our collective future in Canada. As I said at the start of this book, I had a queasy feeling in the pit of my gut telling me Canada — the nation — is in trouble. By reading what I found on my journey, I hope you will agree that my claim was not made with blind ignorance of what is happening to Canada's place in the world.

There is an astounding amount of evidence that suggests Canada is becoming marginalized in the world; we are falling behind the front-runners. As the evidence in this book portrays, there are many circumstances holding Canada back as we head into this 21st century. In many cases, because of the crippling legacies we have left to the next generation of Canadians — debt, high taxes and ineffective political institutions — we have tied the hands of our youth just at the time our youth could endeavour to make our country successful.

It is time to untie those hands.

The only forward-looking vision this country can seem to muster is to try to avoid a complete economic crisis. We have let the dollar slide, we have seen the tax gap between the U.S. and Canada rise, we have seen the U.S. take the high road in creating more highly productive jobs and we have seen our standard of living fall. Not only has Canada not acted to mitigate these trends in any substantial way, in many cases the problem has grown worse.

In the meantime, our political elite, particularly our prime minister himself, seems to have fallen back on creaky notions of nationalism to suggest nothing is wrong. "The UN says we are the best in the world," or "our health-care system will keep people in Canada," or "our softer, gentler society will keep us un-American" are the kind of platitudes still uttered.

Well, folks, I hate to break it to you but that just is not going to fly with young, up-and-coming Canadians. To just say you are "un-American" will not do; you must act to change the economic and political culture to suit your own desires. We simply can't take for granted that the loyalty and allegiance to Canada by its people will remain unquestioned. With a global economy erasing once hard-line geopolitical borders, and careers now being more critical than country, success more sacred than allegiance, Canada had better figure out what it wants to be in this global game. Or the consequence will be that we simply won't matter anymore. We will become someone else's economic backwater.

Unfortunately, the worst part of the problem is that our political institutions do not have the slightest idea of how to fix our country's political and economic malaise.

Anyone who has read this far, I hope, will note that this book is really only a glimpse into one of the symptoms of Canada's marginalization. Based on my seven years of study of Canada's government, I am convinced what I put forward here is only a piece of the puzzle; there is clearly much more to explore. And since I did these interviews I have uncovered more, which will be presented in this series of books and documentaries.

I ask this question: where has Parliament been — our highest governing body where our national interests are supposed to be discussed — as the country has slowly weakened relative to our southern neighbour? Is it not the job of Parliament, those on the government side and the opposition side, to oversee our national views and force our government to act?

Herein lies the problem for our country and where I took my research. For decades, as the evidence in this book shows, the Canadian government has sat by complacently, protecting us from change and opting for the status quo political and government structures that have led us down the road to economic decline. Meanwhile, they do have the tools to stop the rot. There is the possibility that our leadership, through Parliament, could strengthen Canada. Yet Parliament has been silent in overseeing our successive governments.

In my view, Parliament has been an inert body, unable to grasp the magnitude of the problem, and at best only makes short-term political statements about Canada being a global leader by 2010, or that we must become more "innovative," whatever that means. The government's words seldom match its results, while Parliament never holds these governments accountable for the false platitudes they spout.

I can only hope this book and the accompanying documentary have shown that the status quo just will not do. Parliament must get re-engaged in the debate here. It sounds simple enough, but our Parliament, by definition the people whom we elect to represent our interests in Ottawa, needs to be part of our national dialogue again. They — Parliament and the citizen — currently are out of the loop.

We, as a nation, have a choice to change the situation. What will we choose?

POSTSCRIPT

I MUST NOTE THAT I have thought long and hard about how the destruction of the World Trade Center and all the post–September 11, 2001 issues may have influenced what I have reported.

I think there has definitely been more of an effect on the American psyche, and probably not so much of an effect on the psyche of those Canadians who live in the United States. In my observation, the Canadians in the U.S. have already weighed the pros and cons of whatever negative thoughts they may have had of America before they left. Clearly, Canadians see the American lifestyle and its more isolationist and myopic political culture with different eyes than Americans themselves do. These Canadians are in the U.S. because they have seen the strengths of the U.S. as outweighing any reservations they may have had about living there. Over the long run, terrorism will have much less effect on the U.S.'s ability to attract talented people from Canada than the economic culture it has been able to develop.

INDEX